国际贸易实务

Practice of International Trade

主　编　阮晓文　王　莎
副主编　管　俊　宣小箐

哈尔滨工程大学出版社
Harbin Engineering University Press

内容简介

本书共10章，采用全英文形式，以外贸实际业务流程为主线，以职业能力和职业素养为中心，培养学生从事外贸工作的实践能力。

本书是为来华留学生及中外合作办学院校的本科生与专科生而编写，也适合有志于从事国际贸易实际业务的各类外贸人员参考使用。

图书在版编目(CIP)数据

国际贸易实务/阮晓文，王莎主编. —哈尔滨：哈尔滨工程大学出版社，2018.4

ISBN 978-7-5661-2057-1

Ⅰ.①国… Ⅱ.①阮… ②王… Ⅲ.①国际贸易—贸易实务—教材—英文 Ⅳ.①F740.4

中国版本图书馆CIP数据核字(2018)第162988号

选题策划 田 婧
责任编辑 张淑娜
封面设计 刘长友

出版发行 哈尔滨工程大学出版社
社　　址 哈尔滨市南岗区南通大街145号
邮政编码 150001
发行电话 0451-82519328
传　　真 0451-82519699
经　　销 新华书店
印　　刷 北京中石油彩色印刷有限责任公司
开　　本 787 mm×1 092 mm 1/16
印　　张 11.75
字　　数 395千字
版　　次 2018年4月第1版
印　　次 2018年4月第1次印刷
定　　价 45.80元

http://www.hrbeupress.com
E-mail:heupress@hrbeu.edu.cn

Preface

While international trade has existed throughout history, economic, social and political importance has been on the rise in recent centuries.

Trading globally gives consumers and countries the opportunity to be exposed to new markets and products. Almost every kind of product can be found in the international market: food, clothes, spare parts, oil, jewelry, wine, stocks, currencies and water. Services are also traded: tourism, banking, consulting and transportation. A product that is sold to the global market is an export, and a product that is bought from the global market is an import. Exports and imports are accounted for in a country's current account in the balance of payments.

Industrialization, advanced technology, including transportation, globalization, multinational corporations and outsourcing are all having a major impact on the international trade system. Increasing international trade is crucial to the continuance of globalization. Nations would be limited to the goods and services produced within their own borders without international trade. International trade is, in principle, not different from domestic trade as the motivation and the behavior of parties involved in a trade do not change fundamentally regardless of whether trade is across a border or not. The main difference is that international trade is typically more costly than domestic trade. This is due to the fact that a border typically imposes additional costs such as tariffs, time costs caused by border delays, and costs associated with country differences such as language, the legal system, or culture.

This book has 10 chapters which contain the general introduction international trade, business communication, trade terms, payment terms, international cargo transportation, marine cargo insurance, contract and so on.

We hope that the book can help everyone who wants to learn International Trade.

Contents

Chapter One General Introduction on International Trade

This part covers the following topics:

1.1 The Importance of International Trade;
1.2 Theory of Comparative Advantage and Absolute Advantage;
1.3 Types of International Trade;
1.4 Modes of International Trade;
1.5 One-Belt-One-Road Initiative(OBOR);
1.6 China's Cross-Border E-Commerce.

By the end of this part, you will be able to master:

1. Theory of Comparative Advantage, Absolute Advantage, Competitive Advantage;
2. Type of Trade;
3. Modes of International Trade;
4. General Information on China's International Trade;
5. One-Belt-One-Road Initiative;
6. China's Cross-Border Ecommerce.

1.1 The Importance of International Trade

International trade is opening doors to new entrepreneurial opportunity across the world. It also provides a country's people with a greater choice of goods and services. International trade is an important engine for job creation in many countries. From a historical perspective, international trade has grown remarkably in the last couple of centuries. After a long period characterized by persistently low international trade, over the course of the 19th century, technological advances triggered a period of marked growth in world trade (the "first wave of globalization"). This process of growth stopped, and was eventually reversed in the interwar period; but international trade started growing again since the Second World War, and in the last decades trade expansion has been grown faster than ever before. Today, the sum of exports and imports across nations is higher than 50% of global production. At the turn of the 19th century this figure was below 10%. In the last couple of decades, transport and communication costs have decreased across the world, and preferential trade agreements have become more and more common, particularly among developing countries. In fact, trade among developing nations (often referred to as South-South trade), more than tripled in the period 1980 – 2011. Free international trade is often seen as desirable because it allows countries to specialize, in order to produce goods that they are relatively efficient at producing, while importing other goods. This is the essence of the comparative advantage argument supporting gains from trade: exchange allows countries to "do what they do best, and import the rest".

The value and volume of international trade continues to increase. In 2016, the world merchandise exports are valued at more than 15.46 trillion USD, and service exports are nearly over 11 trillion USD. Table 1-1 shows the world largest exporters.

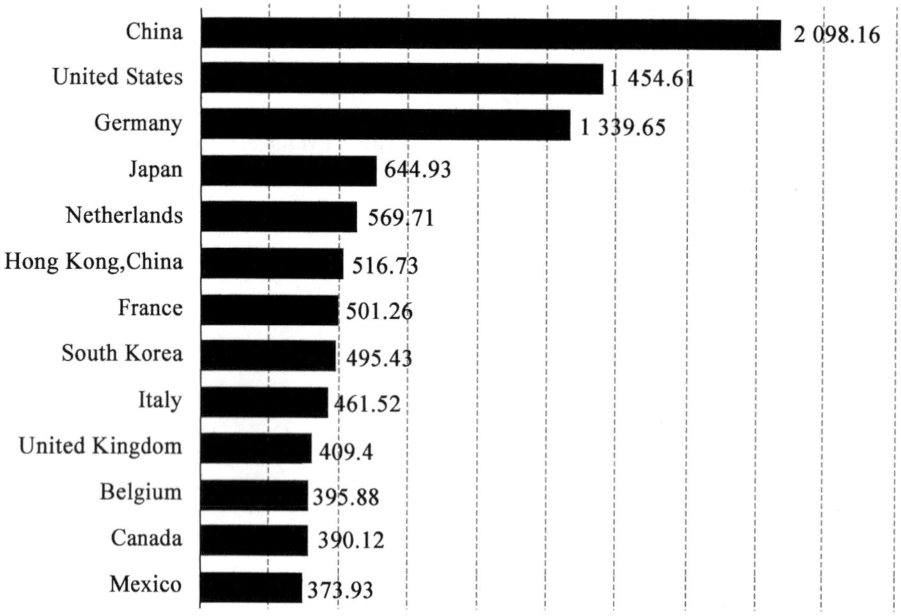

Table 1-1 The world largest exporters

China ranked first in exports with an export value of about 2.1 trillion US dollars. The leading import country in 2016 was the United States with an import value of about 2.25 trillion US dollars. China leads the world in exports in 2016, followed by the United States, with exports valued at 1.45 trillion US dollars, and Germany, with exports valued at 1.34 trillion US dollars.

The value of goods exported from China grew immensely between 2002 and 2014. In 2002, China's exports were valued at about 327 billion US dollars. China's export value grew to 2 trillion US dollars in 2012, the first year in which China exported more than 2 trillion US dollars worth of goods. Year over year export growth remained above 17 percent between 2002 and 2012, except in 2009 and 2012. In 2004, export value grew by over 35 percent. In 2011, China accounted for about 10 percent of global merchandise exports and about 4 percent of global service exports. China's greatest export product category in 2011 was machinery and transport equipment, of which the wroth they exported is 902 billion US dollars. In 2012, China exported 159 billion US dollars worth of clothes and clothing accessories.

International trade has flourished over the years due to the many benefits it has offered to different countries across the globe. International trade is the exchange of services, goods, and capital among various countries and regions, without much hindrance. Global trading provides countries and consumers the chance to be exposed to those services and goods that are not available in their own country. International trading permits the developed countries use their resources effectively like technology, capital and labor. International Trade exerted a profound influence on the economic growth of a country.

The international trade accounts for a good part of a country's gross domestic product. It is also one of important sources of revenue for a developing country.

Some important benefits of International Trade

- Enhances the domestic competitiveness
- Takes advantage of international trade technology
- Increase sales and profits
- Extend sales potential of the existing products
- Maintain cost competitiveness in domestic market
- Enhance potential for expansion of business
- Gains a global market share
- Reduce dependence on existing markets
- Stabilize seasonal market fluctuations

1.2 Theory of Comparative Advantage and Absolute Advantage

1.2.1 Comparative Advantage

The theory of comparative advantage is an economic theory about the work gains from trade for individuals, firms, or nations that arise from differences in their factor endowments or technological progress. In an economic model, agents have a comparative advantage over others in producing a particular good if they can produce that good at a lower relative opportunity cost or autarky price, i. e. at a lower relative marginal cost prior to trade. The closely related law or principle of comparative advantage holds that under free trade, an agent will produce more of and consume less of a good for which they have a comparative advantage.

David Ricardo explained comparative advantage in his 1817 book On the Principles of Political Economy and Taxation in an example involving England and Portugal. In Portugal it is possible to produce both wine and cloth with less labor than it would take to produce the same quantities in England. However, the relative costs of producing those two goods are different in the two countries. In England it is very hard to produce wine, and only moderately difficult to produce cloth. In Portugal both are easy to produce. Therefore while it is cheaper to produce cloth in Portugal than England, it is cheaper still for Portugal to produce excess wine, and trade that for English cloth. Conversely, England benefits from this trade because the cost for producing cloth has not changed but it can now get wine at a lower price, closer to the cost of cloth. The conclusion drawn is that each country can gain by specializing in the good where it has comparative advantage, and trading that good for the other.

A country has a comparative advantage when it is unable to produce a good more efficiently than other nation but produces the good more efficiently than it does any other good. For example, oil-producing nations have a comparative advantage in chemicals. That's because the oil provides a cheap source of material for the chemicals when compared to countries without it. As a result, Saudi Arabia, Kuwait and Mexico compete well with U. S. chemical production firms. That makes their chemicals less expensive. That's because a lot of the raw ingredients are produced in the oil distillery process. Comparative advantage can be derived from economies of scale, more efficient internal systems, location in geographies with low labor or low property expenses. Chinese E-Commerce Giant—Taobao of Alibaba Group is an example of a company focused on building and maintaining comparative advantage. The e-commerce platform, its vendor relationship and its shipping network provide a level of scale and efficiency that is difficult for retail competitors to replicate.

1.2.2 Absolute Advantage

In economics, the principle of absolute advantage refers to the ability of a party (an individual, a firm, or a country) to produce a greater quantity of goods, products, or services than competitors, using the same amount of resources. Adam Smith first described the principle of absolute advantage in the context of international trade, using labor as the only input. A country with an absolute advantage can sell the good for less than a country that does not have the absolute advantage. For example, China export low-cost manufactured goods, which take advantage of much lower unit labor costs. Therefore, a country that has an absolute advantage can produce a good at lower marginal cost and it can sell the good for less than the country that does not have the absolute advantage.

1.2.3 The Differences between Absolute Advantage and Comparative Advantage

Absolute advantage and comparative advantage are two important concepts in international trade. When a nation can make a product at a greater quality and faster rate than another, it has an absolute advantage. Comparative advantage is based on opportunity cost, which is the benefit one forfeits by choosing an alternative option. If one nation has a lower opportunity cost than another to produce a good, it has a comparative advantage. Absolute advantage is the advantage of one country over another if it can produce larger number of goods with the same resources than other countries. On the other hand, comparative advantage is the ability of a country to make a particular item better than other countries. Meanwhile, under absolute advantage, mutually beneficial trade is not possible, comparative advantage provides for mutually beneficial trade between countries.

1.3 Competitive Advantage

Competitive advantage is the attribute that allows an organization to outperform its competitors. A competitive advantage may include access to natural resources, such as high-grade ores or a low-cost power source, highly skilled labor, geographic location, high entry barriers, and access to new technology. Michael Porter defined the two ways in which an organization can achieve competitive advantage over its rivals: cost advantage and differentiation advantage. Cost advantage is when a business provides the same products and services as its competitors, albeit at a lesser cost. Differentiation advantage is when a business provides better products and services as its competitors. In Porter's view, strategic management should be concerned with building and sustaining competitive advantage.

Competitive advantage seeks to address some of the criticisms of comparative advantage. Competitive advantage rests on the notion that cheap labor is ubiquitous and natural resources are not necessary for a good economy. The other theory, comparative advantage, can lead countries to specialize in exporting primary goods and raw materials that trap countries in low-wage economies due to terms of trade.

1.4 Types of International Trade

According to the direction of commodity movement, international trade can be divided into export trade, import trade and transit trade. According to the form of goods, international trade can be divided into visible trade and invisible trade. According to the relations between producer and consumer countries in trade, international trade can be divided into direct trade and indirect trade. According to trade content, international trade can be divided into trade in service, commodity trade, processing trade and general trade. According to the number of participating countries, international trade can be divided into bilateral trade and multilateral trade.

1.4.1 Export

Export means transferring of goods or services produced in one country to another country. The seller of such goods and services is referred to as an exporter; the foreign buyer is referred to as an importer.

1.4.2 Import

An import is a good brought into a jurisdiction, especially across a national border, from an external source. The party bringing in the good is called an importer. An import in the receiving country is an export from the sending country.

1.4.3 Transit Trade

Transit trade means that the goods in country A pass through country C and are finally delivered to country B for sale. For the sake of country C, it is transit trade. (Note: Due to the impeding effect of transit trade on international trade, at present, WTO members are not engaged in cross-border trade.)

1.4.4 Visible Trade and Invisible Trade

Visible trade refers to the exchange of physical goods in every stage of production. They are also known as international merchandise transactions. In economics, visible trade refers to the exchange of physically tangible goods between countries, involving the export, import, and re-export of goods at various stages of production.

In economics, invisible trade refers to the exchange of physically intangible items between countries. Invisible trade can be distinguished from visible trade, which involves the export, import, and re-export of physically tangible goods. Basic categories of invisible trade include services (receipts and payments arising from activities such as customer service or shipping); income from foreign investment in the form of interest, profits and dividends; private or government transfers of monies from one country to another; and intellectual property and patents.

1.4.5 Direct Trade and Indirect Trade

Direct trade is when Country A trades something they have for something Country B has. Indirect trade is when Country A doesn't have something Country B wants, so Country A trades the goods to Country C in order to obtain the goods that Country B wants. Once Country A has the goods of Country C, Country A will then trade with Country B.

1.4.6 Trade in Services

Trade in Services refers to the sale and delivery of an intangible product, called a service, between a producer and consumer. Trade in services takes place between a producer and consumer that are, in legal terms, based in different countries, or economies, which is called International Trade in Services. International Trade in Services is defined by the Four Modes of Supply of the General Agreement on Trade in Services (GATS).

(Mode 1) Cross border trade—which is defined as delivery of a service from the territory of one country into the territory of other country;

(Mode 2) Consumption abroad—this mode covers supply of a service of one country to the service consumer of any other country;

(Mode 3) Commercial presence—which covers services provided by a service supplier of one country in the territory of any other country;

(Mode 4) Presence of natural persons—which covers services provided by a service supplier of one country through the presence of natural persons in the territory of any other country.

1.4.7 Commodity Trade

Commodity trade refers to the purely business-oriented trading activities for the purpose of buying and selling commodities. Such transactions include some specific transactions such as distribution (distribution, exclusive distribution, special distribution and general distribution), agency (general agent, exclusive agent, special agent and general agent), consignment, auction, tenders and exhibitions and other sales.

1.4.8 Processing Trade

Processing trade refers to the business activities of importing all or part of raw and auxiliary materials, parts, components and packaging materials imported by the operating enterprises and re-exporting finished products after processing or assembly, including processing of imported materials and processing of raw materials. Processing trade is a re-export business characterized by processing. According to different business characteristics, the common processing trade modes include feed processing, material processing, assembly business and collaborative production.

1.4.9 General Trade

General trade refers to the trade of unilateral import or unilateral export of enterprises which have the right to import and export in China and the goods imported and exported in this way are generally traded goods. General trade goods is also a kind of customs supervision goods. The Customs Law of China stipulates that when the goods or the vehicles of transport enter or leave the country, the consignee or consignor or his agent must request the Customs at the entry and exit points to declare; they have to submit required documents and receive the customs inspection; and then pay customs duties and other taxes; finally, the Customs can approve the release of goods and means of transport.

1.4.10 Bilateral Trade and Multilateral Trade

Bilateral trade or clearing trade is trade exclusively between two states, particularly, barter trade based on bilateral deals between governments, and without using hard currency for payment. Bilateral trade agreements often aim to keep trade deficits at minimum by keeping a clearing account where deficit would accumulate. Bilateral trade agreements are the agreements between two nations for the purpose of exchange of goods and service each other for mutual benefit of both of the countries. Under bilateral trade agreements; the exchange of agreements takes place in commercial relationship, trade facilitation, finance investment etc. So the trade between both of countries makes simple by simple procedures of imports and exports, cutting down or minimizing the taxes or duties on overseas trade etc. The ultimate aim of any bilateral trade agreement between countries is to improve the economic status of both of the countries. Compared to multilateral agreements, bilateral agreements are easy to negotiate with terms and conditions of agreements.

Multilateral trade agreements are made between two or more countries to strengthen economy of member countries by exchanging of goods and services among them. The multilateral trade agreement builds commercial relationship, trade facilitation and financial investments among member countries of such multilateral trade agreement. Compared to bilateral trade agreement, multilateral trade agreements are difficult in negotiation of agreement, as more member countries are involved in multilateral trade agreements. Up to the level of norms in multilateral trade agreement, the member countries are treated equally. The multilateral trade agreements can be formed in regional basis also. There are many multilateral trade agreements between countries worldwide regionally for the development of economy of each member countries signed in each multilateral trade agreement.

1.4.11 Trade Barriers

Trade barriers refer to government laws, regulations, policy, or practices that either protect domestic products from foreign competition or artificially stimulate exports of particular domestic products. The most common foreign trade barriers are government-imposed measures and policies that restrict, prevent, or impede the international exchange of goods and services.

1.4.12 Trade Tariffs

A tariff is a tax placed on a specific good or set of goods exported from or imported to a country, creating an economic barrier to trade. Taking an example, one country wants to protect its failing industries, then the country places the tariff on the industry. As a result, the industry is less enticed to produce goods in a quicker, cheaper, and more productive fashion. There is another reason for a country to place heavy tariff which may involve the issue of dumping. Dumping involves a country producing highly excessive amounts of goods and dumping the goods on another country which will cause a result of destroy the country's related industries. Dumping may refer to either pricing the good from the foreign market at a price lower than charged in the domestic market of the country of origin or refers to the producer selling the product at a price in which there is no profit or a loss. The purpose and expected outcome of the tariff is to encourage the development of domestic industries.

1.4.13 Balance of Trade

The balance of trade, commercial balance, or net exports (sometimes symbolized as NX), is the difference between the monetary value of a nation's exports and imports over a certain period. Sometimes a distinction is made between a balance of trade for goods versus one for services. If a country exports a greater value than it imports, it is called a trade surplus, positive balance, or a "favorable balance", and conversely, if a country imports a greater value than it exports, it is called a trade deficit, negative balance, "unfavorable balance", or, informally, a "trade gap".

1.5 Licensing

Licensing refers to a technology licensor transacts the use right of the subject matter of the transaction to the technology receiver through a license agreement or contract. It is also known as "licensed trade". The subject matter of the permit, which is usually "soft technology", can be a patent, a design, an industrial model, a trademark and copyright, or a know-how. Licensing allows the licensor to use its patents, trademarks or know-how by the licensor; the licensor pays fees and other remuneration to the licensor as consideration for the use of its technology. Licensing has combined the "revolution in science and technology, the accumulation of knowledge and the revolution in industrial applications" to speed up the process of product life cycle and technology life cycle. Developing countries can use the licensing to obtain greater economic benefits with smaller investments, shorten the technological gap and enjoy the benefits of technological progress. The exporters can recoup investment in research and risk costs.

1.6 Modes of International Trade

With the rapid development of international trade, the mode of trade has also undergone great changes. In addition to the traditional way of import and export of commodities, there are exclusive sales, agent, consignment, auction, tender and so on. In recent years, counter trade, processing trade, and other trade methods are widely used.

1.6.1 Exclusive Sales

Exclusive sales refer to the exporter and foreign companies who signed an agreement to sell commodity sales authority only to a particular foreign client or company. The foreign client or company will have the right to sell and manage the goods for a certain period of time limit. The exclusive sales agreement is entirely a contract of sale, because foreign client or company need to buy goods in their own name and take the risk of operation.

1.6.2 Agent

Agent refers to an independent person or legal entity, which acts on behalf of another ("Principal"). In international transactions, this term normally refers to a sales representative who prospects on behalf of a foreign principal, earning a commission on sales eventually concluded between the principal and the ultimate client. This is distinguished from sales through employees and subsidiaries—that are not independent—or through distributors buying and reselling in his or her own name. In international trade, relationships between agents and their clients are regulated through a Model of International Agency Contract.

1.6.3 Consignment

Consignment is the act of consigning, the act of giving over to another person or agent's charge, custody or care any material or goods but retaining legal ownership until the material or goods are sold. It may be done for the purpose of shipping the goods, transferring the goods to auction or intending the goods to be placed on sale in a store.

1.6.4 Auction

An auction is a process of buying and selling goods or services by offering them up for bid, taking bids, and then selling the item to the highest bidder. The open ascending price auction is arguably the most common form of auction in use today. Participants bid openly against one another, with each subsequent bid required to be higher than the previous bid.

1.6.5 Tender

To tender is to invite bids for a project, or to accept a formal offer such as a takeover bid. Tender usually refers to the process whereby governments and financial institutions invite bids for large projects that must be submitted within a finite deadline. The term also refers to the process whereby shareholders submit their shares or securities in response to a takeover offer.

1.6.6 Counter Trade

Counter trade means exchanging goods or services which are paid for, in whole or part, with other goods or services, rather than with money. A monetary valuation can be used in counter trade for accounting purposes. There are six main variants of counter trade:

1. Barter

Exchange of goods or services directly for other goods or services without the use of money as means of purchase or payment. Barter is the direct exchange of goods between two parties in a transaction. The principal exports are paid for with goods or services supplied from the importing market. A single contract covers both flows, in its simplest form involves no cash. In practice, supply of the principal exports is often held up until sufficient revenues have been earned from the sale of bartered goods. One of the largest barter deals to date involved Occidental Petroleum Corporation's agreement to ship sulphuric acid to the former Soviet Union for ammonia urea and potash under a 2 year deal which worth 18 billion Euros. Furthermore, at negotiation stage of a barter deal, the seller must know the market price for items offered in trade. Bartered goods can range from hams to iron pellets, mineral water, furniture or olive-oil all somewhat more difficult to price and market when potential customers must be sought.

2. Switch trading

Practice in which one company sells to another its obligation to make a purchase in a given country.

3. Counter purchase

Sale of goods and services to one company in other country by a company that promises to make a future purchase of a specific product from the same company in that country.

4. Buyback

It occurs when a firm builds a plant in a country—or supplies technology, equipment, training, or other services to the country and agrees to take a certain percentage of the plant's output as partial payment for the contract.

5. Offset

Agreement that a company will offset a hard-currency purchase of an unspecified product from that nation in the future. Agreement by one nation to buy a product from another, subject to the purchase of some or all of the components and raw materials from the buyer of the finished product, or the assembly of such product in the buyer nation.

6. Compensation trade

Compensation trade is a form of barter in which one of the flows is partly in goods and partly in hard currency.

1.6.7 Processing Trade

Processing trade refers to the business activity of importing all or part of the raw and auxiliary materials, parts and components, accessories, and packaging materials from abroad in bond, and re-exporting the finished products after processing or assembly by enterprises within the mainland. It includes processing with supplied materials and imported materials. Under processing with supplied materials, the imported materials and parts are supplied by the foreign party which is also responsible for selling the finished products. The business enterprise does not have to make foreign exchange payment for the imports and only charges the foreign party a processing fee. Under processing with imported materials, the business enterprise makes foreign exchange payment for the imported materials and parts and exports the finished products after processing.

1.6.8 Overseas Processing and Assembling Trade

There are several types of overseas processing and assembling trade. It mainly includes original equipment manufacturer(OEM), original design manufacturer(ODM) and original brand manufacturer(OBM).

An original equipment manufacturer is a company that produces parts and equipment that may be marketed by another manufacturer. For example, if Acme Manufacturing Co. makes power cords that are used on IBM computers, Acme is an OEM.

An original design manufacturer is a company that designs and manufactures a product, as specified, that is eventually rebranded by another firm for sale. Such companies allow the firm that owns or licenses the brand to produce products (either as a supplement or solely) without having to engage in the organization or running of a factory. ODMs have grown in size in recent years and as of 2015 many have the scale to handle production in-house for the products that are branded by the buying firm. This is in contrast to a contract manufacturer (CM).

This model is especially used in international trade, where a local ODM is used to produce goods for a foreign company that sees some advantages in the transaction, such as low labor-inputs, transport links or proximity to markets.

An original brand manufacturer, or OBM, is typically a company that sells the entire product made by a second company or including a component from a second company sources as its own branded product. Selling the product of the second company under its own brand just adds a virtual extrinsic value to the product.

1.7 General Introduction on China's International Trade

China was the world's largest exporter from 2013 to 2015, it exported MYM 2 trillion of its production in 2016. China was the world's greatest exporter of computers, broadcasting equipment, telephones, office machine parts, insulated wire, video displays, rubber tires, low-voltage protection equipment, valves and semiconductor devices. Other major exports included electrical transformers, furniture, knit sweaters, trunks and cases, video displays, vehicle parts, seats, insulated wire and video recording equipment. Other major imports of China included soybeans, refined petroleum, LCDs, refined copper, coal briquettes, vehicle parts, computers, petroleum gas and copper ore.

The top 5 export destinations of China were the United States, Hong Kong SAR, Japan, South Korea and Germany. The top 4 import origins were Hong Kong SAR, the United States,

Japan and Germany.

China is the world's third largest importer. In 2016, it imported MYM 1.4 trillion. China imported raw commodities from Latin America and Africa, such as oil and other fuels, metal ores, plastics and organic chemicals. It was the world's largest importer of aluminum and copper. China's commodity consumption has fueled a world-wide boom in mining and agriculture. By the end of 2016, China approved a cumulative of 864,304 foreign investment projects, with actual utilized overseas FDI amounting to USMYM 1,765.5 billion.

China's foreign exchange reserves stood at USMYM 3,109.2 billion by the end of October. 2017, was the largest in the world. In 2015, FDI made by Chinese enterprises in overseas markets reached USMYM 145.7 billion. In 2016, China's outward FDI grew by 34.7% to USMYM 196.2 billion, ranked as the second largest source after the US. As at the end of 2016, China's stock of outward FDI reached USMYM 1,357.4 billion, ranked the sixth in the world. Business services, financial services, wholesale and retail, mining and manufacturing are the leading sectors of China's outward FDI.

1.8 One-Belt-One-Road Initiative (OBOR)

The Silk Road Economic Belt and the 21st-century Maritime Silk Road, better known as the One-Belt-One-Road Initiative (OBOR), The Belt and Road (B&R) and The Belt and Road Initiative (BRI) is a development strategy proposed by China's leader Xi Jinping that focuses on connectivity and cooperation among Eurasian countries, primarily China, the land-based Silk Road Economic Belt and the oceangoing Maritime Silk Road. The strategy underlines China's push to take a larger role in global affairs with a China-centered trading network. It was unveiled in September and October 2013. In the past years until 2016, the focuses were mainly on infrastructure investment, construction materials, railway and highway, automobile, real estate, power grid, and iron and steel.

The Belt and Road initiative is geographically structured along 6 corridors, and the maritime silk road.

- New Eurasian Land Bridge, running from Western China to Western Russia through Kazakhstan.
- China – Mongolia – Russia Corridor, running from Northern China to Eastern Russia.
- China – Central Asia – West Asia Corridor, running from Western China to Turkey.
- China – Indochina Peninsula Corridor, running from Southern China to Singapore.
- China – Myanmar – Bangladesh – India Corridor, running from Southern China to Myanmar.
- China – Pakistan Corridor, running from South – Western China to Pakistan.
- Maritime Silk Road, running from the Chinese Coast through Singapore to the Mediterranean.

"Belt and Road" is expected to build a new global economic and trade cycle, and become the third largest economic development space after the Atlantic and Pacific Oceans. The "Belt and Road" region covers a total population of about 4.6 billion (more than 60% of the world's population), with a total GDP of 20 trillion U. S. dollars (accounting for about one third of the world's population). In 2015, the amount of service outsourcing contracts to be undertaken by China under the "Belt and Road Initiative" amounted to 17.83 billion U.S. dollars. The total import and export volume of the countries along the "Belt and Road" in 2016 was 6,257.17 billion yuan.

By the end of 2016, Chinese enterprises had built 56 economic and trade cooperation zones in more than 20 countries along the "One Belt and One Road", with a total investment of over 18.5 billion U.S. dollars. China created nearly 1.1 billion U.S. dollars of tax revenue and 180,000 jobs for the host country.

The Asian Infrastructure Investment Bank, first proposed by China in October 2013, is a development bank dedicated to lending for projects regarding infrastructure. As of 2015, China announced that over one trillion yuan (MYM 160 billion US) of infrastructure projects were in planning or construction. It is opened in 2016 and its membership expanded from 57 when it was first established to 77; in 2014, China proposed the establishment of a Silk Road Fund. As of December 2017, the Silk Road Fund has signed 17 projects, committed to invest about 7 billion U.S. dollars and the total investment involved in supporting the project amounts to 80 billion U.S. dollars.

1.9 China's Cross-Border E-Commerce

China has become a front runner in E-commerce and online retail. China's rapid economic growth combined with the swift development of the internet has proved to be a profitable coincidence for the powerhouse country. China has the world's largest online population growth, putting it on track to rake in MYM 650 billion in online sales by the year 2020. China has been the largest retail e-commerce market in the world. Online retailing is expected to grow from 17% of total retail sales in 2017 to 25% by 2020. China today is characterized by mobile—first consumer behavior and vibrant social commerce adoption. Taobao, part of the Alibaba Group, is the largest online shopping site in Asia with upwards of 500 million registered users.

According to the monitoring data of China E-Commerce Research Center, the trading scale of China's cross-border electricity supplier market in 2012 – 2016 was 2.1 trillion yuan in 2012, 3.15 trillion yuan in 2013, 4.2 trillion yuan in 2014, 5.4 trillion yuan in 2015, 6.7 trillion yuan in 2016. Data showed that in the past five years, China's cross-border electricity market transactions increased 4.6 trillion yuan. In 2012 – 2016, the scale of transactions in China's livelihood e-commerce market was 153 billion yuan in 2012, 213 billion yuan in 2013, 310 billion yuan in 2014, 445 billion yuan in 2015 and 760 billion yuan in 2016. The data showed that in the past five years, the transaction amount of e-commerce in China's living services has increased by 607 billion yuan. Cross-border e-commerce has increasingly been a mainstream way in international trade in China. Chinese companies are combining online trade with offline promotions. Chinese consumers are purchasing international products through online without travelling abroad. In the past years, there is an amazing growth, led by JD worldwide, Tmall Global, and specialty platform Netease Kaola. It is reported that the total revenue of cross-border e-commerce in 2016 was 6.7 trillion yuan. It increased 24% than 2015. The total revenue of export of e-commerce was 5.5 trillion yuan and the total revenue of import e-commerce reached 1.2 trillion yuan. It is expected that the total volume can reach 7.5 trillion yuan in 2017 and there will be 58 million users are expected to engage in cross-border transactions in 2017. Chinese consumers would like to purchase through Netease Kaola (24.2%), Tmall Global (20.3%), Vip. com (15.7%), JD Worldwide (12.5%), YMatou. com (5.8%), Little Red Book (5.3%) and Mia. com (3.1%). It is reported that Japan, Germany, Korea, France and America are top destinations for Chinese cross-border purchase.

China has 10 pilot cities for cross-border e-commerce including Shanghai, Hangzhou, Ningbo, Zhengzhou, Chongqing Guangzhou, Shenzhen, Tianjin, Fuzhou and Pingtan where international business is conducted as "bonder import" or "direct purchase import".

Exercises

I. Multiple Choice

1. China ranked first in exports with an export value of about ________ US dollars in 2016.

A. 1.6 trillion B. 2.1 trillion

C. 2.5 trillion D. 2.6 trillion

2. ________ refers to the exchange of physical goods in every stage of production.

A. Invisible trade B. Visible trade

C. Bilateral trade D. International Trade

3. There are six main variants of counter trade including Barter, Offset, Buyback, Counter purchase, Switch trading and ________.

A. Compensation trade B. Bilateral trade

C. Invisible trade D. Visible trade

4. There are several types of overseas processing and assembling trade. It mainly includes OEM, ODM and ________.

A. OBM B. OCM

C. ODE D. WTO

5. According to different business characteristics, the common processing trade modes include feed processing, material processing, assembly business and ________.

A. collaborative production B. multilateral production

C. transit production D. counter production

6. ________ is a tax placed on a specific good or set of goods exported from or imported to a country, creating an economic barrier to trade.

A. A tariff B. A commission

C. Discount D. Duty

7. ________ agreements are made between two or more countries to strengthen economy of member countries by exchanging of goods and services among them.

A. Bilateral trade
B. Multilateral trade
C. Free trade
D. Processing trade

8. ________ refers to a technology licensor transacts the use right of the subject matter of the transaction to the technology receiver through a license agreement or contract.

A. Copyright
B. Paten
C. Licensing
D. Branding

II. True or False

1. Commodity trade refers to the purely business-oriented trading activities for the purpose of buying and selling commodities. ( )

2. An original design manufacturer (ODM) is a company that designs and manufactures a product, as specified, that is eventually rebranded by another firm for sale. ( )

3. Developing countries are not permitted to use the licensing to obtain greater economic benefits with smaller investments. ( )

4. Trade tariff refer to government laws, regulations, policy, or practices that either protect domestic products from foreign competition or artificially stimulate exports of particular domestic products. ( )

5. In international transactions, agent refers to a sales representative who prospects on behalf of a foreign principal, earning a commission on sales. ( )

6. The Belt and Road initiative is geographically structured along 5 corridors, and the maritime silk road. ( )

7. A country has an absolute advantage when it is unable to produce a good more efficiently than other nation. ( )

8. According to the number of participating countries, international trade can be divided into: bilateral trade and multilateral trade. ( )

9. To tender is to invite bids for a project, or to accept a formal offer such as a takeover bid. ( )

10. Counter trade means exchanging goods or services which are paid for, in whole or part, with other goods or services, rather than with money. ( )

III. Questions

1. What is the importance of international trade?

2. What are the differences between theory of Comparative Advantage and Absolute Advantage?

3. How many types of international trade are there?

4. How many modes of international trade are there?

5. What is One-Belt-One-Road Initiative?

Chapter Two Business Communication

This part covers the following topics:

2.1 Business Negotiation;
2.2 Essential Elements of an Export Contract.

By the end of this part, you will be able to master:

1. Market research;
2. Negotiation strategies;
3. Enquiry letters;
4. Offering letters;
5. Counter offering letters;
6. Acceptance letters;
7. International trade contracts.

2.1 Business Negotiation

Negotiation is a process where two or more parties with different needs and goals discuss an issue to find a mutually acceptable solution. In business, negotiation skills are important in both informal day-to-day interactions and formal transactions such as negotiating conditions of sale, lease, service delivery, and other legal contracts. Negotiating requires give and take. Business negotiation is a process of planning, organizing, leading and controlling to achieve an organization goals and objectives. Furthermore, it also acts as a medium to bargain with another business partner or business rival. The more public relation skills we possess the better we can negotiate.

2.1.1 Market Research

Market research is any organized effort to gather information about target markets or customers. It is a very important component of business strategy. Factors that can be investigated through market research include:

1. Market information

Through market information one can know the prices of different commodities in the market, as well as the supply and demand situation.

2. Market segmentation

Market segmentation is widely used for segmenting on geographic differences, personality differences, demographic differences, techno-graphic differences, use of product differences, psychographic differences and gender differences.

3. Market trends

Market trends are the upward or downward movement of a market, during a period of time.

4. SWOT analysis

SWOT is a written analysis of the Strengths, Weaknesses, Opportunities and Threats to a business entity. Not only should a SWOT be used in the creation stage of the company, but also be used throughout the life of the company.

2.1.2 Negotiation Strategies

1. Be prepared

The most important step in successful negotiations is to be fully prepared first. Knowledge of goods, knowledge of markets and prices, knowledge of supply and demand, understanding of the company, understanding of each other, the company's bottom line, targets, caps, and other objectives of negotiation must be prepared; meanwhile you need to list the priorities on paper and keep them informed as you negotiate.

2. Avoiding negotiations from breaking down

Experienced salesmen will not let the negotiations be completely broken or they will not have to negotiate at all. He will always leave each other a little retreat until an agreement is reached at the next negotiation.

3. To be a good listener

In general, business people always think they are articulate and prefer to speak. Negotiators should try their best to let them talk more. From their speaking and body language, it is possible to find out their advantages and disadvantages as well as understand their negotiating position.

4. Put yourself in the business for the sake of partners

Only few people in the world think that negotiations should be done without any concessions. Facts have proved that most successful procurement negotiations are possible in a harmonious atmosphere. Everyone values "face-saving", and nobody wants to negotiate in a threatening atmosphere. Moreover, the company should have a steady partnership with good suppliers rather than a confrontational relationship.

5. Prepare multiple negotiation plans

Both parties initially proposed the plans which were very beneficial to themselves. On the other hand, both parties want to gain more benefits through negotiations. Therefore, the outcome of the negotiations will certainly not be the original plan put forward by the two sides, but through consultation, compromise and flexibility between the two sides. The best way we need to do is to prepare several sets of negotiation plans and come up with the most favorable plan.

6. Concessional attack

In the process of negotiation, one or two very high demands can be put forward in due time. The other party will inevitably disagree. After some bargaining, we can make concessions and reduce or change them. As far as these high demands, we initially did not intend to reach an agreement, even if concessions were not lost. However, it gives opponents a sense of accomplishment and feels that they gained comparative advantage. In this case, it is easy to be accepted by the other party when the request is lower than the high requirement. However, it is forbidden to make the request too outrageous or excessive, otherwise the other party may think that we are not sincere and even angered them.

2.1.3 Enquiry in International Trade

1. Enquiries

An enquiry is a request for business information, such as price lists, catalogue, samples, and details about the goods or trade terms. It can be made by either the importer or exporter. Enquiries can be divided into general enquiries and specific enquiries.

General enquiries: for general information—information about various goods.

Specific enquiries: for specific information—stronger intension to make an order.

Sample letters:

Letter 2 - 1

Dear Sirs,

We have noted from www. alibaba. com that you are dealing in fashion accessories.

Being specialized in this line, we are experienced and well connected with many customers at our end.

We shall be grateful if you will send us the latest illustrated catalogues and price lists. If possible, please airmail us some free samples in order to acquaint us with the quality and workmanship of your supplies.

If the goods and trade terms prove satisfactory, you may expect from us substantial orders in the future.

We look forward to your early response.

Yours faithfully

Letter 2 - 2

Dear Sirs,

Our customers are interested in your electric stand fans and ask us to approach you for quotations and samples of goods available for export now.

We shall be very appreciated if you will quote us your lowest price CIPC 5% Los Angeles for 20,000 pieces of the captioned products, indicating the earliest date of shipment and payment terms.

For your information, competition from similar makes is very keen here. Please see to it that your price is in line with the current market so that we can secure more orders for you.

We anticipate receiving your early reply.

Yours Faithfully

2. Replies for enquiries

Any international trade company which received an enquiry will write back.

Sample letters:

Letter 2 - 3

Dear Mr. Amir,

Many thanks for your inquiry dated(of) × × × × from alibaba. com.

In order to lct us make more correct quotation accordingly, please kindly tell us the exact model number you prefer after checking our website of http://www. abc. com. cn.

Besides, to help us offer the best price, please also introduce your company as more details as you can. Such as your company foundation time, how many workers, major product lines, company website and last year's sales turnover if possible. More details better price.

Waiting for your early reply.

Best Regards

Amy

Letter 2 - 4

Dear Mr. Naresh,

So glad receiving your enquiry for our Barbies' collection from Alibaba. com dated × × ×. Thanks a lot.

Our enterprise is a leading manufacturer in children's wear in China and our products have been exported to customers all over the world such as * * * *. The Barbies Collection is the most popular style in our factory, selling fast.

However, detailed price list for the skirts and long pants will be sent to you based on your specific further product description such as color, specification, special design requirement etc. Please check the following styles photo which should be suitable for your Indian market and tell us more

requirements on the exact skirts and long pants.
Please do not hesitate to contact us if you have any question and we are waiting for your reply.
Best regards,
Amy

2.1.5 Offer

In international trade, a proposal that is made to a foreign individual or legal entity to enter into a contract, that is definitive in its terms, and that indicates the offer's intent to be bound by acceptance.

1. Basic conditions of an offer

The basic conditions of an offer include:

(1) The offer shall be made to one more specific people.

(2) Contents of the offer shall be sufficiently definite; trade terms of the offer shall be complete, clear and finalized.

(3) The offer shall indicate the intention of the offerer to be bound in case of acceptance.

2. Time of the validity or duration of an offer

(1) Stipulate the latest date for acceptance.

(2) Stipulate a period of time for acceptance.

(3) Arrival theory.

3. Offer with engagement and offer without engagement

(1) Offer with engagement means the offerer's intention of reaching a contract is definitely indicated, which is also called "firm offer" "irrevocable offer".

(2) It should include: detailed description of the item price, currency, packaging, minimum or maximum quantity, quality, shipping date, mode, terms of payment.

(3) Offer without engagement means an offer which is unclear, incompleted or being with reservations. It is not binding upon both parties.

Sample letters:

Letter 2 – 5

Dear Sirs,
This is to confirm your fax of May 12th, 2014, asking us to make you firm offer for rice and soybeans CFR Singapore.
We faxed you this morning, offering 300 metric tons of polished rice at US MYM 2500 per metric ton, CFR Singapore, for shipment during Nov. 2014. This offer is firm, subject to the receipt of your reply here before October 1st.
Please note that we have quoted our most favorable price and are unable to entertain any counter

offer.

With regard to soybeans, we advise you that the few lots we have at present are under offer elsewhere. If, however, you should make us an acceptable bid, there is a possibility of our supplying them.

As you know, of late, there has been a heavy demand for these commodities and this has resulted in increased prices. You may, however, take advantage of the uptrend market price if you send an immediate reply.

Yours faithfully

Letter 2 – 6

Dear Sirs,

We are pleased to know from your E-mail of yesterday that you are interested in our products, especially Vitamin E. We are now making you an offer as follows, subject to your replay reaching here before 21st, May.

Commodity: Vitamin E 50% F. C. C.

Price: US MYM 8.5 per kg CIF Shanghai

Quantity: 5000 kg

Packing: 25 kg/ drum

Shipping mark: At seller's option

Date of shipment: Nov. 2014

Payment: By irrevocable L/C at sight, to reach us one month before shipment date, allowing transshipment and partial shipments.

Insurance: To be effected by seller for 110% of full invoice value covering All Risks, War Risk and Strike Risk.

Looking forward to your early confirmation.

Yours faithfully

4. Counter-offer

An offer made in response to a previous offer by the other party during negotiations for a final contract. Making a counter offer automatically rejects the prior offer, and requires an acceptance under the terms of the counter offer or there is no contract.

Sample letters:

Letter 2 – 7

Dear Sirs,

Re: Hainan Mangos, 2014 Crop

We are in receipt of your E-mail of yesterday, offering us 50 metric tons of the captioned goods at EUR 1200/MT CIP Amsterdam.

In reply, we regret to inform you that the buyers at our end find your price to be on the high side. Information indicates that some parcels of Indian origin have been sold here at a level about 15%

lower than yours.
We do not deny that the quality of Hainan Mangos is slightly better, but the difference in price should, in no case, be as big as 15%.
To step up trade, we, on behalf of our buyers, make the following counteroffer, subject to your reply reaching us by May 31st, our time.
"50 metric tons of Mangos, 2014 crop at EUR 1050/MT CIP Amsterdam, other terms as per your E-mail dated May 18th, 2014."
As the market price is falling, we recommend your immediate acceptance.
Your faithfully

Letter 2 - 8
Dear Sirs,
Re: Hainan Mangos, 2014 Crop
We are informed in your mail of May 20th that our price for the above article is found on the high side, since Indian products are being offered to you at a price approximately 15% lower than that quoted by us.
Although we do not doubt about what you say, we are of the opinion that the quality of other origins does not measure up to that of our products. Desirous as we are to expand our business in West Europe, we feel very regretful that we cannot accept your counteroffer or even meet you half way. The best we can do is to make a reduction of 5% in our previous quotation. We hope you will direct the attention of your customers to the superior quality of our products and reconsider the prices we quoted.
We look forward to hearing from you soon.
Yours faithfully

2.1.6 Acceptance

An offeree's agreement to the terms set by the offerer is called an "Acceptance". An acceptance, which should be expressed and unconditional, should reach the offerer within the validity of the offer.

Sample letter:
Letter 2 - 9
Dear Sirs,
Thank you for your letter of May 18th for cotton shirts. We are pleased to inform you that we accept your counteroffer.
Please note, however, that we have specially accepted your request solely because we wish to make this the forerunner of many future orders from you.
We hope you will send us your formal order by return, which we will execute with our best attention.

Yours very truly

2.2 Essential Elements of an Export Contract

The export contract is used for the international sale of certain products (industrial supplies, raw materials, manufactured goods), which are projected for resale, where the buyer is a trader, importer, distributor or wholesaler that will sell the products to another company or merchant. Though it is common practice to export products based a proforma invoice or quotation received from exporters, it is a safe practice to use written and legal export contracts.

It is difficult to draw up a comprehensive contract that can be standardized for all export transactions. However, the exporter and the importer should be aware of certain minimum general requirements when drawing up an export sales contract. The clauses covering these requirements will make up the basic elements of the contract and are outlined below:

- Name and addresses of the parties. State clearly and fully the parties to the contract.
- Product, standards and specifications. State the product name, as well as technical names (if any); sizes in which the product is to be supplied (if relevant); applicable national or international standards and specifications; specific buyer requirements; and sample specifications.
- Quantity. Specify units of measure in both figures and words.
- Inspection. State the nature, manner and focus of the envisaged inspection, as well as the inspection agency. A number of goods are now subject to pre-shipment inspection by designated agencies, and foreign buyers may stipulate their own inspection agencies and conditions for inspection.
- Total value. State the total contract value in words and figures, and specify the currency.
- Terms of delivery. State the delivery terms, based on one of the Incoterms 1990. Note: a new version of Incoterms will be applicable on 1 January 2000.
- Taxes, duties and charges. Clarify responsibility for all taxes. The prices quoted by the seller may be inclusive of taxes, duties, and charges. Levies in the country of importation (if any) may be the buyer's responsibility.
- Delivery. Specify the place of dispatch and delivery. Also state whether the period of delivery will run from the date of the contract, from the date of notification of the issue of an irrevocable letter of credit, or from the date of receipt of the notice of issuance of the import license by the seller.
- Part-shipment, trans-shipment and consolidation of cargo. State whether the parties to the contract have agreed on part-shipment or trans-shipment. Indicate the port of trans-shipment and the number, if any, of partial shipments agreed. If the goods are likely to be shipped under a "consolidation of export cargos" scheme, mention this in the contract.
- Packaging, labeling and marking. Note all packaging, labeling and marking requirements in the contract.

- Terms of payment: amount, mode and currency. When quoting different payment terms, the exporter should specify whether the prices are based on the current rate of exchange of in-country currency, or on the basis of another currency (such as US dollars). Address payment terms for exchange rate fluctuations as well.
- Discounts and commissions. Specify the amount of discount or commission to be paid and by whom (by the exporter or by the importer). Stipulate the basis of calculation of commission and rate to be applied. Discount or commission rates may or may not be included in the export price agreed upon by the exporter and importer.
- Licenses and permits. State whether the export transaction will require any export or import licenses, and whose responsibility and expense it will be to obtain them. Import licenses may be difficult to obtain in the buyer's country.
- Insurance. A contract should provide for the insurance of goods against loss, damage, or destruction during transportation. Specify the type of risk covered and the extent of coverage.

Sample of Export Contract

Seller: Yang Pu Co. Ltd., China
Buyer: Pearson Co. Ltd., America
Contact Information: Ship to: 16#. Emperor Road, New York
15#, Songze Road, Pudong, Shanghai
Purchase Oder: No. LBS20170806
Date: 08/10/2017
Terms of Price: CIF New York Port

Number	Description	Quantity	Area/m^2	Price US $/$m^2$	Amount US $
1	Thermal Transfer Ribbon SD-180 (Resin) Size: 910 mm (Film Width) × about 16,500 m/roll	5 Rolls	32,000	0.16	5,120
2	Thermal Transfer Ribbon SDC-220K (Resin for Care lable) Size: 910 mm (Film width) × about 13,800 m/roll	2 Rolls	25,000	0.26	6,500
Amount				Total	11,620
TOTAL AMOUNT: * * * * * *					

Remarks

1. +/-20% more or less in quantity and amount should be acceptable.
2. Measure of area, and so on, subject to the final confirmation.

3. ALL GOODS ARE SUBJECT TO INSPECTION AFTER DELIVERY. WE RESERVE THE RIGHT TO

REJECT ANY MATERIAL OR GOODS WHICH ARE PROVED TO BE FAULTY IN DESIGN, QUALITY

CONSTRUCTION, OR WHICH DO NOT COPME UP TO THE SAMPLE OR STANDARD SPECIFIED.

4. PAYMENT: by advance TT remittance

5. DELIVERY DATE: 08/30/2017

6. B/L should be confirmed by consignee.

7. The packing of the goods shall be preventive from dampness, rust, moisture, erosion and shock, and shall be suitable for ocean transportation/multiple transportation. The Seller shall be liable for any damage and loss of the goods attributable to the inadequate or improper packing. The measurement, gross weight, net weight and the cautions such as "Do not stack up side down" "Keep away from moisture" "Handle with care" shall be stenciled on the surface of each package with fadeless pigment.

8. Documents Required:

8.1 Full set of clean on board Ocean/Combined Transportation/Land Bills of Lading and blank endorsed marked freight prepaid/to collect.

8.2 Signed commercial invoice in __2__ copies indicating Contract No. and shipping marks;

8.3 Packing list/weight memo in __2__ copies issued by shipper;

8.4 Insurance policy/certificate in __2__ copies (Terms of CIF);

8.5 The Seller shall, within 48 hours after shipment effected, send by courier each copy of the above-mentioned documents.

9. The Seller shall ship the goods duly within the shipping duration from the port of loading to the port of destination.

10. The Seller shall, immediately upon the completion of the loading of the goods, advise the Buyer of the Contract No., names of commodity, loading quantity, invoice values, gross weight, name of vessel and shipment date by fax or email within 48 hours.

11. This Contract is in __2__ copies, effective since being signed/sealed by both parties.

- The Seller: The Buyer:
  Date: Date:

2.2.5 Documentary Requirements

Modern international trade is completed mostly in the form of delivery against documents or payment against documents. Therefore, it is of special importance to make good documents in the export business in order to assure the timely and safe payment.

Documents needed for international trade transactions include four categories:

- Documents for export and subsequent import of goods.

- Documents for the buyer to take delivery of the goods.
- Documents relating to payment.
- Special documents required by the nature of the goods, and conditions of sale (e. g., certain engineering goods may involve documents relating to construction, repair and maintenance).

Common export documents include the bill of exchange; commercial invoice and other invoices; bill of lading or airway bill; insurance policy; and letter of credit.

2.2.6 Other Elements

- **Product guarantee**: fix and specify the length of the period of guarantee.
- **Delay in delivery**: define the damages due to the buyer from the seller in the event of late delivery owing to reasons other than force majeure.
- **Force majeure or excuse for non-performance of contract**: provisions in the contract defining the circumstances which would relieve partners of their liability for non-performance of the contract; such provisions are called force majeure and are intended to identify the relief which may be available to either party to the contract should supervening circumstances occur during the period of validity of the contract.
- **Remedial action**: as defaults in contractual obligations by any of the parties can occur, it is always advisable to include in the sale or purchase contract certain specific remedial actions; these remedial actions should reflect the mandatory provisions of the law applicable to the contract.
- **Applicable law**: state the law of the country which is to govern the contract.
- **Arbitration**: facilitate amicable and quick settlement of disputes or differences that may arise between the parties.
- **Signature of the parties**: the signing of the contract indicates the agreement of both parties to the terms and conditions of the contract.

2.3 Export and Import Procedures

2.3.1 Export Procedure

As for China's export trade, although FOB terms are sometimes being used for large transactions, most of the transactions are completed on CIF and CFR terms. To implement the contract and assure the contract being performed satisfactorily, necessary procedures shall be fulfilled as follows.

- Examining L/C
- Preparation of Products
- Applying Mandatory Inspection

- Receiving Importer's Inspection
- Booking Shipping Space
- Clearing Goods for Export
- Getting Goods Loaded
- Obtaining Insurance
- Presenting Documents for Bank Negotiation

2.3.2 Import Procedure

Once the import contract is concluded in accordance with the law, both the seller and buyer must be in strict accordance with the provisions of the contract and fulfill their contractual obligations. The relevant import procedures are involved as follows.

- Opening Letter of Credit
- Booking Shipping Space
- Obtaining Insurance
- Examining Documents and Making Payment
- Clearing Goods for Import
- Taking Delivery and Inspecting

2.4 Disputes and Claims

It takes a long time to fulfill the whole process of international trade because it relates to a wide range of business links. It is possible to meet some accidents or make some mistakes such as the production of the goods, the purchase of the goods, transportation and capital movement, it may bring negative impact on the accomplishment of the contract. With unpredictable change of the international market and many unforeseen factors, one party might often fail to accomplish the contract or perform all the obligations under the contract, which may result in the damage the interest of the other party. It leads to disputes and claims.

2.4.1 Settlement of Disputes

The contract signed for the international sale of goods is the legal document concerning the sale of the rights and obligations of both parties. If any party fails to perform the contract obligations, or rendered non-conforming performance, which constitutes a breach in the law, the defaulting party shall be liable to perform, to take remedial measures, or to compensate for losses. According to provisions of national laws and the provisions of international treaties, the breach is different, the responsibility varies.

2.4.2 Settlement of Disputes Between Nations

Resolving trade disputes is one of the core activities of the WTO. A dispute arises when one member country adopts a trade policy measure or takes some action that one or more fellow members considers to a breach of WTO agreements or to be a failure to live up to obligations. The WTO has one of the most active international dispute settlement mechanisms in the world.

Exercises

I. Multiple Choice

1. A SWOT analysis is divided into: ________.

A. Strength, Weakness, Opportunities and Thoughts

B. Strength, Weakness, Opportunities and Threats

C. Sickness, Weakness, Offer and Threats

D. Strength, Weakness, Offer and Threats

2. Market Research is composed of ________.

A. Market segmentation, Market information, Market trends and SWOT analysis

B. Market weakness, Market strength, Market trends and SWOT analysis

C. Market segmentation, Market weakness, Market threats and Market orientation

D. Market segmentation, Market threats, Market analysis and Market trends

3. Time of the Validity or Duration of an Offer including the following contents except: ________.

A. stipulate the latest date for acceptance

B. stipulate a period of time for acceptance

C. arrival theory

D. efficiency

4. Business negotiation is a process of planning, organizing, ________ to achieve an organization goals and objectives.

A. leading and controlling

B. dividing and controlling

C. trying and leading

D. controlling and breaking

5. Common export documents include the bill of exchange, commercial invoice and other invoices, bill of lading or airway bill, insurance policy and ________.

A. letter of credit　　B. letter of offer

C. letter of acceptance　　D. letter of counter-offer

6. Offer with engagement means the offerer's intention of reaching a contract is definitely indicated, which is also called "firm offer" or ________.

A. “irrevocable offer”
B. “counter-offer”
C. “refund offer”
D. “double-offer”

II. True or False

1. It is a safe practice to use written and legal export contracts. (　　)

2. As for China's export trade, although FOB terms are sometimes being used for large transactions, most of the transactions are completed on CIF and CFR terms. (　　)

3. Offer without engagement means an offer which is unclear, incompleted or being with reservations. It is binding upon both parties. (　　)

4. It is not difficult to draw up a comprehensive contract that can be standardized for all export transactions. (　　)

5. Arbitration can facilitate amicable and quick settlement of disputes or differences that may arise between the parties. (　　)

6. An enquiry is a request for business information, such as price lists, catalogue, samples, and details about the goods or trade terms. (　　)

7. A dispute arises when one member country adopts a trade policy measure or takes some action that one or more fellow members considers to a breach of WTO agreements. (　　)

8. Discount or commission rates may or may not be included in the export price agreed upon by the exporter and importer. (　　)

9. When quoting different payment terms, the exporter should specify whether the prices are based on the current rate of exchange of in-country currency. (　　)

10. Delay in delivery defines the damages due to the buyer from the seller in the event of late delivery owing to reasons other than force majeure. (　　)

III. Questions

1. What are main steps for business negotiation?
2. What is a counter-offer?
3. What is the essential elements of an export contract?
4. Describe the import procedure?
5. Describe the export procedure?

Chapter Three International Trade Terms

This part covers the following topics:

3.1 The Introduction to Incoterms® 2010 rules;

3.2 The 11 Incoterms® 2010 rules.

By the end of this part, you will be able to master the following terms:

1. EXW
2. FCA
3. CPT
4. CIP
5. DAT
6. DAP
7. DDP
8. FAS
9. FOB
10. CFR
11. CIF

3.1 The Introduction to Incoterms® 2010 Rules

The Incoterms® rules have become an essential part of the daily language of trade. They have been incorporated in contracts for the sale of goods worldwide and provide rules and guidance to importers, exporters, lawyers, transporters, insurers and students of international trade. Here are main features of the Incoterms® 2010 rules.

3.1.1 Two New Incoterms Rules—DAT and DAP—Have Replaced the Incoterms 2000 Rules DAF, DES, DEQ and DDU

The number of Incoterms® rules has been reduced from 13 to 11. This has been achieved by substituting two new rules that may be used irrespective of the agreed mode of transport—DAT, Delivered at Terminal, and DAP, Delivered at Place—for the Incoterms® 2000 rules DAF, DES, DEQ and DDU. Under both new rules, delivery occurs at a named destination: in DAT, at the buyer's disposal unloaded from the arriving vehicle (as under the former DEQ rule); in DAP, likewise at the buyer's disposal, but ready for unloading (as under the former DAF, DES and DDU rules). The new rules make the Incoterms® 2000 rules DES and DEQ superfluous. The named terminal in DAT may well be in a port, and DAT can therefore safely be used in cases where the Incoterms® 2000 rule DEQ once was. Likewise, the arriving "vehicle" under DAP may well be a ship and the named place of destination may well be a port: consequently, DAP can safely be used in cases where the Incoterms® 2000 rule DES once was. These new rules, like their predecessors, are "delivered", with the seller bearing all the costs (other than those related to import clearance, where applicable) and risks involved in bringing the goods to the named place of destination.

3.1.2 Classification of the 11 Incoterms® 2010 Rules

The 11 Incoterms® 2010 rules are presented in two distinct classes:

(1) RULES FOR ANY MODE OR MODES OF TRANSPORT:

EXW EX WORKS

FCA FREE CARRIER

CPT CARRIAGE PAID TO

CIP CARRIAGE AND INSURANCE PAID TO

DAT DELIVERED AT TERMINAL

DAP DELIVERED AT PLACE

DDP DELIVERED DUTY PAID

(2) RULES FOR SEA AND INLAND WATERWAY TRANSPORT

FAS FREE ALONGSIDE SHIP

FOB FREE ON BOARD

CFR COST AND FREIGHT

CIF COST INSURANCE AND FREIGHT

The first class includes the seven Incoterms® 2010 rules that can be used irrespective of the mode of transport selected and irrespective of whether one or more than one mode of transport is employed. EXW, FCA, CPT, CIP, DAT, DAP and DDP belong to this class. They can be used even when there is no maritime transport at all. It is important to remember, however, that these rules can be used in cases where a ship is used for part of the carriage.

In the second class of Incoterms® 2010 rules, the point of delivery and the place to which the goods are carried to the buyer are both ports, hence the label "sea and inland waterway" rules. FAS, FOB, CFR and CIF belong to this class. Under the last three Incoterms rules, all mention of the ship's rail as the point of delivery has been omitted in preference for the goods being delivered when they are "on board" the vessel. This more closely reflects modern commercial reality and avoids the rather dated image of the risk swinging to and fro across an imaginary perpendicular line.

3.1.3 Rules for Domestic and International Trade

Incoterms® rules have traditionally been used in international sale contracts where goods pass across national borders. In various areas of the world, however, trade blocs, like the European Union, have made border formalities between different countries less significant. Consequently, the subtitle of the Incoterms® 2010 rules formally recognizes that they are available for application to both international and domestic sale contracts. As a result, the Incoterms® 2010 rules clearly state in a number of places that the obligation to comply with export/import formalities exists only where applicable. Two developments have persuaded the ICC that a movement in this direction is timely. Firstly, traders commonly use Incoterms® rules for purely domestic sale contracts. The second reason is the greater willingness in the United States to use Incoterms® rules in domestic trade rather than the former Uniform Commercial Code shipment and delivery terms.

3.2 The 11 Incoterms® 2010 Rules

3.2.1 EXW—EX Works

This rule may be used irrespective of the mode of transport selected and may also be used where more than one mode of transport is employed. It is suitable for domestic trade, while FCA is usually more appropriate for international trade.

"Ex Works" means that the seller delivers when it places the goods at the disposal of the buyer at the seller's premises or at another named place (i. e., works, factory, warehouse, etc.). The seller does not need to load the goods on any collecting vehicle, nor does it need to clear the goods for export, where such clearance is applicable.

The parties are well advised to specify as clearly as possible the point within the named place of delivery, as the costs and risks to that point are for the account of the seller. The buyer bears all costs and risks involved in taking the goods from the agreed point, if any, at the named place of delivery.

EXW represents the minimum obligation for the seller. The rule should be used with care as:

a) The seller has no obligation to the buyer to load the goods, even though in practice the seller may be in a better position to do so. If the seller does load the goods, it does so at the buyer's risk and expense. In cases where the seller is in a better position to load the goods, FCA, which obliges the seller to do so at its own risk and expense, is usually more appropriate.

b) A buyer who buys from a seller on an EXW basis for export needs to be aware that the seller has an obligation to provide only such assistance as the buyer may require to effect that export: the seller is not bound to organize the export clearance. Buyers are therefore well advised not to use EXW if they cannot directly or indirectly obtain export clearance.

c) The buyer has limited obligations to provide to the seller any information regarding the export of the goods. However, the seller may need this information for, e. g., taxation or reporting purposes.

A. THE SELLER'S OBLIGATIONS

A1. General obligations of the seller

The seller must provide the goods and the commercial invoice in conformity with the contract of sale and any other evidence of conformity that may be required by the contract.

Any document referred to in A1 – A10 may be an equivalent electronic record or procedure if agreed between the parties or customary.

A2. Licences, authorizations, security clearances and other formalities

Where applicable, the seller must provide the buyer, at the buyer's request, risk and expense, assistance in obtaining any export licence, or other official authorization necessary for the export of the goods.

Where applicable, the seller must provide, at the buyer's request, risk and expense, any information in the possession of the seller that is required for the security clearance of the goods.

A3. Contracts of carriage and insurance

a) Contract of carriage

The seller has no obligation to the buyer to make a contract of carriage.

b) Contract of insurance

The seller has no obligation to the buyer to make a contract of insurance. However, the seller must provide the buyer, at the buyer's request, risk and expense (if any), with information that the buyer needs for obtaining insurance.

A4. Delivery

The seller must deliver the goods by placing them at the disposal of the buyer at the agreed point, if any, at the named place of delivery, not loaded on any collecting vehicle. If no specific point has been agreed within the named place of delivery, and if there are several points available, the seller may select the point that best suits its purpose. The seller must deliver the goods on the agreed date or within the agreed period.

A5. Transfer of risks

The seller bears all risks of loss of or damage to the goods until they have been delivered in accordance with A4 with the exception of loss or damage in the circumstances described in B5.

A6. Allocation of costs

The seller must pay all costs relating to the goods until they have been delivered in accordance with A4, other than those payable by the buyer as envisaged in B6.

A7. Notices to the buyer

The seller must give the buyer any notice needed to enable the buyer to take delivery of the goods.

A8. Delivery document

The seller has no obligation to the buyer.

A9. Checking – packaging – marking

The seller must pay the costs of those checking operations (such as checking quality, measuring, weighing, and counting) that are necessary for the purpose of delivering the goods in accordance with A4.

The seller must, at its own expense, package the goods, unless it is usual for the particular trade to transport the type of goods sold unpackaged. The seller may package the goods in the manner appropriate for their transport, unless the buyer has notified the seller of specific packaging requirements before the contract of sale is concluded. Packaging is to be marked appropriately.

A10. Assistance with information and related costs

The seller must, where applicable, in a timely manner, provide to or render assistance in obtaining for the buyer, at the buyer's request, risk and expense, any documents and information, including security-related information, that the buyer needs for the export and/or import of the goods and/or for their transport to the final destination.

B. THE BUYER'S OBLIGATIONS

B1. General obligations of the buyer

The buyer must pay the price of the goods as provided in the contract of sale.

Any document referred to in B1 – B10 may be an equivalent electronic record or procedure if agreed between the parties or customary.

B2. Licences, authorizations, security clearances and other formalities

Where applicable, it is up to the buyer to obtain, at its own risk and expense, any export and import licence or other official authorization and carry out all customs formalities for the export of the goods.

B3. Contracts of carriage and insurance

a) Contract of carriage

The buyer has no obligation to the seller to make a contract of carriage.

b) Contract of insurance

The buyer has no obligation to the seller to make a contract of insurance.

B4. Taking delivery

The buyer must take delivery of the goods when A4 and A7 have been complied with.

B5. Transfer of risks

The buyer bears all risks of loss of or damage to the goods from the time they have been delivered as envisaged in A4.

If the buyer fails to give notice in accordance with B7, then the buyer bears all risks of loss of or damage to the goods from the agreed date or the expiry date of the agreed period for delivery, provided that the goods have been clearly identified as the contract goods.

B6. Allocation of costs

The buyer must:

a) pay all costs relating to the goods from the time they have been delivered as envisaged in A4;

b) pay any additional costs incurred by failing either to take delivery of the goods when they have been placed at its disposal or to give appropriate notice in accordance with B7, provided that the goods have been clearly identified as the contract goods;

c) pay, where applicable, all duties, taxes and other charges, as well as the costs of carrying out customs formalities payable upon export; and

d) reimburse all costs and charges incurred by the seller in providing assistance as envisaged in A2.

B7. Notices to the seller

The buyer must, whenever it is entitled to determine the time within an agreed period and/or the point of taking delivery within the named place, give the seller sufficient notice thereof.

B8. Proof of delivery

The buyer must provide the seller with appropriate evidence of having taken delivery.

B9. Inspection of goods

The buyer must pay the costs of any mandatory pre-shipment inspection, including inspection mandated by the authorities of the country of export.

B10. Assistance with information and related costs

The buyer must, in a timely manner, advise the seller of any security information requirements so that the seller may comply with A10.

The buyer must reimburse the seller for all costs and charges incurred by the seller in providing or rendering assistance in obtaining documents and information as envisaged in A10.

3.2.2 FCA—Free Carrier

This rule may be used irrespective of the mode of transport selected and may also be used where more than one mode of transport is employed.

"Free Carrier" means that the seller delivers the goods to the carrier or another person nominated by the buyer at the seller's premises or another named place. The parties are well advised to specify as clearly as possible the point within the named place of delivery, as the risk passes to the buyer at that point.

If the parties intend to deliver the goods at the seller's premises, they should identify the address of those premises as the named place of delivery. If, on the other hand, the parties intend the goods to be delivered at another place, they must identify a different specific place of delivery.

FCA requires the seller to clear the goods for export, where applicable. However, the seller has no obligation to clear the goods for import, pay any import duty or carry out any import customs formalities.

A. THE SELLER'S OBLIGATIONS

A1. General obligations of the seller

The seller must provide the goods and the commercial invoice in conformity with the contract of sale and any other evidence of conformity that may be required by the contract.

Any document referred to in A1 – A10 may be an equivalent electronic record or procedure if agreed between the parties or customary.

A2. Licences, authorizations, security clearances and other formalities

Where applicable, the seller must obtain, at the its own risk and expense, any export licence, or other official authorization carry out all customs formalities necessary for the export of the goods.

A3. Contracts of carriage and insurance

a) Contract of carriage

The seller has no obligation to the buyer to make a contract of carriage. However, if requested by the buyer or if it is commercial practice and the buyer does not give an instruction to the contrary in due time, the seller may contract for carriage on usual terms at the buyer's risk and expense. In either case, the seller may decline to make the contract of carriage and, if it does, shall promptly notify the buyer.

b) Contract of insurance

The seller has no obligation to the buyer to make a contract of insurance. However, the seller must provide the buyer, at the buyer's request, risk and expense (if any), with information that the buyer needs for obtaining insurance.

A4. Delivery

The seller must deliver the goods to the carrier or another person nominated by the buyer at the agreed point, if any at the named place on the agreed date or within the named period.

Delivery is completed:

a) if the named place is the seller's premises, when the goods have been loaded on the means of transport provide by the buyer.

b) In any other case, when the goods are placed at the disposal of the carrier or another person nominated by the buyer on the seller's means of transport ready for unloading.

If no specific point has been notified by the buyer under B7 d) within the named place of delivery, and if there are several points available, the seller may select the point that best suits its purpose.

Unless the buyer notifies the seller otherwise, the seller may deliver the goods for carriage in such a manner as the quantity and/or nature of the goods may require.

A5. Transfer of risks

The seller bears all risks of loss of or damage to the goods until they have been delivered in accordance with A4, with the exception of loss or damage in the circumstances described in B5.

A6. Allocation of costs

The seller must pay

a) all costs relating to the goods until they have been delivered in accordance with A4, other than those payable by the buyer as envisaged in B6; and

b) where applicable, the costs of customs formalities necessary for export, as well as all duties, taxes, and other charges payable upon export.

A7. Notices to the buyer

The seller must, at the buyer's risk and expense, give the buyer sufficient notice either that the goods have been delivered in accordance with A4 or that the carrier or another person nominated by the buyer has failed to take the goods within the time agreed.

A8. Delivery document

The seller must provide the buyer, at the seller's expense, with the usual proof that the goods have been delivered in accordance with A4.

The seller must provide assistance to the buyer, at the buyer's request, risk and expense, in obtaining a transport document.

A9. Checking – packaging – marking

The seller must pay the costs of those checking operations (such as checking quality, measuring, weighing, and counting) that are necessary for the purpose of delivering the goods in accordance with A4, as well as the costs of any pre-shipment inspection mandated by the authority of the country of export.

The seller must, at its own expense, package the goods, unless it is usual for the particular trade to transport the type of goods sold unpackaged. The seller may package the goods in the manner appropriate for their transport, unless the buyer has notified the seller of specific packaging requirements before the contract of sale is concluded. Packaging is to be marked appropriately.

A10. Assistance with information and related costs

The seller must, where applicable, in a timely manner, provide to or render assistance in obtaining for the buyer, at the buyer's request, risk and expense, any documents and information, including security-related information, that the buyer needs for the export and/or import of the goods and/or for their transport to the final destination.

B. THE BUYER'S OBLIGATIONS

B1. General obligations of the buyer

The buyer must pay the price of the goods as provided in the contract of sale.

Any document referred to in B1 – B10 may be an equivalent electronic record or procedure if agreed between the parties or customary.

B2. Licences, authorizations, security clearances and other formalities

Where applicable, it is up to the buyer to obtain, at its own risk and expense, any import licence or other official authorization and carry out all customs formalities for the import of the goods and for their transport through any country.

B3. Contracts of carriage and insurance

a) Contract of carriage

The buyer must contract at its own expense for the carriage of the goods from the named place of delivery, except when the contract of carriage is made by the seller as provided for in A3 a).

b) Contract of insurance

The buyer has no obligation to the seller to make a contract of insurance.

B4. Taking delivery

The buyer must take delivery of the goods when they have been delivered as envisaged in A4.

B5. Transfer of risks

The buyer bears all risks of loss of or damage to the goods from the time they have been delivered as envisaged in A4.

If

a) the buyer fails in accordance with B7 to notify the nomination of a carrier or another person as envisaged in A4 or to give notice; or

b) the carrier or person nominated by the buyer as envisaged in A4 fails to take the goods into its charge, then, the buyer bears all risks of loss of or damage to the goods:

(i) from the agreed date, or in the absence of an agreed date,

(ii) from the date notified by the seller under A7 within the agreed period; or, if no such date has been notified,

(iii) from the expiry date of any agreed period for delivery, provided that the goods have been clearly identified as the contract goods.

B6. Allocation of costs

The buyer must pay

a) all costs relating to the goods from the time they have been delivered as envisaged in A4, except, where applicable, the costs of customs formalities necessary for export, as well as all duties, taxes, and other charges payable upon export as referred to in A6 b);

b) any additional costs incurred, either because:

(i) the buyer fails to nominate a carrier or another person as envisaged in A4, or

(ii) the carrier or person nominated by the buyer as envisaged in A4 fails to take the goods into its charge, or

(iii) the buyer has failed to give appropriate notice in accordance with B7, provided that the goods have been clearly identified as the contract goods; and

c) where applicable, all duties, taxes and other charges as well as the costs of carrying out customs formalities payable upon import of the goods and the costs for their transport through any country.

B7. Notices to the seller

The buyer must notify the seller of

a) the name of the carrier or another person nominated as envisaged in A4 within sufficient time as to enable the seller to deliver the goods in accordance with that article;

b) where necessary, the selected time within the period agreed for delivery when the carrier or person nominated will take the goods;

c) the mode of transport to be used by the person nominated;

d) the point of taking delivery within the named place.

B8. Proof of delivery

The buyer must accept the proof of delivery provided as envisaged in A8.

B9. Inspection of goods

The buyer must pay the costs of any mandatory pre-shipment inspection, except when such inspection is mandated by the authorities of the country of export.

B10. Assistance with information and related costs

The buyer must, in a timely manner, advise the seller of any security information requirements so that the seller may comply with A10.

The buyer must reimburse the seller for all costs and charges incurred by the seller in providing or rendering assistance in obtaining documents and information as envisaged in A10.

The buyer must, where applicable, in a timely manner, provide to or render assistance in obtaining for the seller, at the sell's request, risk and expense, any documents and information, including security-related information, that the seller needs for the transport and export of the goods and for their transport through any country.

3.2.3 CPT—Carriage Paid To

This rule may be used irrespective of the mode of transport selected and may also be used where more than one mode of transport is employed.

"Carriage Paid To" means that the seller delivers the goods to the carrier or another person nominated by the seller at an agreed place (if any such place is agreed between the parties) and that the seller must contract for and pay the costs of carriage necessary to bring the goods to the named place of destination.

When CPT, CIP, CFR or CIF are used, the seller fulfils its obligation to deliver when it hands the goods over to the carrier and not when the goods reach the place of destination.

This rule has two critical points, because risk passes and costs are transferred at different places. The parties are well advised to identify as precisely as possible in the contract both the place of delivery, where the risk passes to the buyer, and the named place of destination to which the seller must contract for the carriage. If several carriers are used for the carriage to the agreed destination and the parties do not agree on a specific point of delivery, the default position is that risk passes when the goods have been delivered to the first carrier at a point entirely of the seller's choosing and over which the buyer has no control. Should the parties wish the risk to pass at a later stage (e. g., at an ocean port or airport), they need to specify this in their contract of sale.

The parties are also well advised to identify as precisely as possible the point within the agreed place of destination, as the costs to that point are for the account of the seller. The seller is advised to procure contracts of carriage that match this choice precisely. If the seller incurs costs under its contract of carriage related to unloading at the named place of destination, the seller is not entitled to recover such costs from the buyer unless otherwise agreed between the parties.

CPT requires the seller to clear the goods for export, where applicable. However, the seller has no obligation to clear the goods for import, pay any import duty or carry out any import customs formalities.

A. THE SELLER'S OBLIGATIONS

A1. General obligations of the seller

The seller must provide the goods and the commercial invoice in conformity with the contract of sale and any other evidence of conformity that may be required by the contract.

Any document referred to in A1 – A10 may be an equivalent electronic record or procedure if agreed between the parties or customary.

A2. Licences, authorizations, security clearances and other formalities

Where applicable, the seller must obtain, at its own risk and expense, any export licence or other official authorization and carry out all customs formalities necessary for the export of the goods, and for their transport through any country prior to delivery.

A3. Contracts of carriage and insurance

a) Contract of carriage

The seller must contract or procure a contract for the carriage of the goods from the agreed point of delivery, if any, at the place of delivery to the named place of destination or, if agreed, any point at that place. The contract of carriage must be made on usual terms at the seller's expense and provide for carriage by the usual route and in a customary manner. If a specific point is not agreed or is not determined by practice, the seller may select the point of delivery and the point at the named place of destination that best suit its purpose.

b) Contract of insurance

The seller has no obligation to the buyer to make a contract of insurance. However, the seller must provide the buyer, at the buyer's request, risk, and expense (if any), with information that the buyer needs for obtaining insurance.

A4. Delivery

The seller must deliver the goods by handing them over to the carrier contracted in accordance with A3 on the agreed date or within the agreed period.

A5. Transfer of risks

The seller bears all risks of loss of or damage to the goods until they have been delivered in accordance with A4, with the exception of loss or damage in the circumstances described in B5.

A6. Allocation of costs

The seller must pay

a) all costs relating to the goods until they have been delivered in accordance with A4, other than those payable by the buyer as envisaged in B6;

b) the freight and all other costs resulting from A3 a), including the costs of loading the goods and any charges for unloading at the place of destination that were for the seller's account under the contract of carriage; and

c) where applicable, the costs of customs formalities necessary for export, as well as all duties, taxes and other charges payable upon export, and the costs for their transport through any country that were for the seller's account under the contract of carriage.

A7. Notices to the buyer

The seller must notify the buyer that the goods have been delivered in accordance with A4.

The seller must give the buyer any notice needed in order to allow the buyer to take measures that are normally necessary to enable the buyer to take the goods.

A8. Delivery document

If customary or at the buyer's request, the seller must provide the buyer, at the seller's expense, with the usual transport document [s] for the transport contracted in accordance with A3.

This transport document must cover the contract goods and be dated within the period agreed for shipment. If agreed or customary, the document must also enable the buyer to claim the goods from the carrier at the named place of destination and enable the buyer to sell the goods in transit by the transfer of the document to a subsequent buyer or by notification to the carrier.

When such a transport document is issued in negotiable form and in several originals, a full set of originals must be presented to the buyer.

A9. Checking – packaging – marking

The seller must pay the costs of those checking operations (such as checking quality, measuring, weighing, counting) that are necessary for the purpose of delivering the goods in accordance with A4, as well as the costs of any pre-shipment inspection mandated by the authority of the country of export. The seller must, at its own expense, package the goods, unless it is usual for the particular trade to transport the type of goods sold unpackaged.

The seller may package the goods in the manner appropriate for their transport, unless the buyer has notified the seller of specific packaging requirements before the contract of sale is concluded. Packaging is to be marked appropriately.

A10. Assistance with information and related costs

The seller must, where applicable, in a timely manner, provide to or render assistance in obtaining for the buyer, at the buyer's request, risk and expense, any documents and information, including security-related information, that the buyer needs for the import of the goods and/or for their transport to the final destination.

The seller must reimburse the buyer for all costs and charges incurred by the buyer in providing or rendering assistance in obtaining documents and information as envisaged in B10.

B. THE BUYER'S OBLIGATIONS

B1. General obligations of the buyer

The buyer must pay the price of the goods as provided in the contract of sale.

Any document referred to in B1 – B10 may be an equivalent electronic record or procedure if agreed between the parties or customary.

B2. Licences, authorizations, security clearances and other formalities

Where applicable, it is up to the buyer to obtain, at its own risk and expense, any import licence or other official authorization and carry out all customs formalities for the import of the goods and for their transport through any country.

B3. Contracts of carriage and insurance

a) Contract of carriage

The buyer has no obligation to the seller to make a contract of carriage.

b) Contract of insurance

The buyer has no obligation to the seller to make a contract of insurance. However, the buyer must provide the seller, upon request, with the necessary information for obtaining insurance.

B4. Taking delivery

The buyer must take delivery of the goods when they have been delivered as envisaged in A4 and receive them from the carrier at the named place of destination.

B5. Transfer of risks

The buyer bears all risks of loss of or damage to the goods from the time they have been delivered as envisaged in A4.

If the buyer fails to give notice in accordance with B7, it must bear all risks of loss of or damage to the goods from the agreed date or the expiry date of the agreed period for delivery, provided that the goods have been clearly identified as the contract goods.

B6. Allocation of costs

The buyer must, subject to the provisions of A3 a), pay

a) all costs relating to the goods from the time they have been delivered as envisaged in A4, except, where applicable, the costs of customs formalities necessary for export, as well as all duties, taxes, and other charges payable upon export as referred to in A6 c);

b) all costs and charges relating to the goods while in transit until their arrival at the agreed place of destination, unless such costs and charges were for the seller's account under the contract of carriage;

c) unloading costs, unless such costs were for the seller's account under the contract of carriage;

d) any additional costs incurred if the buyer fails to give notice in accordance with B7, from the agreed date or the expiry date of the agreed period for dispatch, provided that the goods have been clearly identified as the contract goods; and

e) where applicable, all duties, taxes and other charges, as well as the costs of carrying out customs formalities payable upon import of the goods and the costs for their transport through any country, unless included within the cost of the contract of carriage.

B7. Notices to the seller

The buyer must, whenever it is entitled to determine the time for dispatching the goods and/or the named place of destination or the point of receiving the goods within that place, give the seller sufficient notice thereof.

B8. Proof of delivery

The buyer must accept the transport document provided as envisaged in A8 if it is in conformity with the contract.

B9. Inspection of goods

The buyer must pay the costs of any mandatory pre-shipment inspection, except when such inspection is mandated by the authorities of the country of export.

B10. Assistance with information and related costs

The buyer must, in a timely manner, advise the seller of any security information requirements so that the seller may comply with A10.

The buyer must reimburse the seller for all costs and charges incurred by the seller in providing or rendering assistance in obtaining documents and information as envisaged in A10.

The buyer must, where applicable, in a timely manner, provide to or render assistance in obtaining for the seller, at the seller's request, risk and expense, any documents and information, including security-related information, that the seller needs for the transport and export of the goods and for their transport through any country.

3.2.4 CIP—Carriage and Insurance Paid To

This rule may be used irrespective of the mode of transport selected and may also be used where more than one mode of transport is employed.

"Carriage and Insurance Paid to" means that the seller delivers the goods to the carrier or another person nominated by the seller at an agreed place (if any such place is agreed between the parties) and that the seller must contract for and pay the costs of carriage necessary to bring the goods to the named place of destination.

The seller also contracts for insurance cover against the buyer's risk of loss of or damage to the goods during the carriage. The buyer should note that under CIP the seller is required to obtain insurance only on minimum cover. Should the buyer wish to have more insurance protection, it will need either to agree as much expressly with the seller or to make its own extra insurance arrangements.

When CPT, CIP, CFR or CIF are used, the seller fulfils its obligation to deliver when it hands the goods over to the carrier and not when the goods reach the place of destination.

This rule has two critical points, because risk passes and costs are transferred at different places. The parties are well advised to identify as precisely as possible in the contract both the place of delivery, where the risk passes to the buyer, and the named place of destination to which the seller must contract for carriage. If several carriers are used for the carriage to the agreed destination and the parties do not agree on a specific point of delivery, the default position is that risk passes when the goods have been delivered to the first carrier at a point entirely of the seller's choosing and over which the buyer has no control. Should the parties wish the risk to pass at a later stage (e. g., at an ocean port or an airport), they need to specify this in their contract of sale.

The parties are also well advised to identify as precisely as possible the point within the agreed place of destination, as the costs to that point are for the account of the seller. The seller is advised to procure contracts of carriage that match this choice precisely. If the seller incurs costs under its contract of carriage related to unloading at the named place of destination, the seller is not entitled to recover such costs from the buyer unless otherwise agreed between the parties.

CIP requires the seller to clear the goods for export, where applicable. However, the seller has no obligation to clear the goods for import, pay any import duty or carry out any import customs formalities.

A. THE SELLER'S OBLIGATIONS

A1. General obligations of the seller

The seller must provide the goods and the commercial invoice in conformity with the contract of sale and any other evidence of conformity that may be required by the contract.

Any document referred to in A1 – A10 may be an equivalent electronic record or procedure if agreed between the parties or customary.

A2. Licences, authorizations, security clearances and other formalities

Where applicable, the seller must obtain, at its own risk and expense, any export licence or other official authorization and carry out all customs formalities necessary for the export of the goods and for their transport through any country prior to delivery.

A3. Contracts of carriage and insurance

a) Contract of carriage

The seller must contract or procure a contract for the carriage of the goods from the agreed point of delivery, if any, at the place of delivery to the named place of destination or, if agreed, any point at that place. The contract of carriage must be made on usual terms at the seller's expense and provide for carriage by the usual route and in a customary manner. If a specific point is not agreed or is not determined by practice, the seller may select the point of delivery and the point at the named place of destination that best suit its purpose.

b) Contract of insurance

The seller must obtain at its own expense cargo insurance complying at least with the minimum cover as provided by Clauses (C) of the Institute Cargo Clauses (LMA/IUA) or any similar clauses. The insurance shall be contracted with underwriters or an insurance company of good repute and entitle the buyer, or any other person having an insurable interest in the goods, to claim directly from the insurer.

When required by the buyer, the seller shall, subject to the buyer providing any necessary information requested by the seller, provide at the buyer's expense any additional cover, if procurable, such as cover as provided by Clauses (A) or (B) of the Institute Cargo Clauses (LMA/IUA) or any similar clauses, and/or cover complying with the Institute War Clauses and/or Institute Strikes Clauses (LMA/IUA) or any similar clauses.

The insurance shall cover, at a minimum, the price provided in the contract plus 10% (i.e., 110%) and shall be in the currency of the contract. The insurance shall cover the goods from the point of delivery set out in A4 and A5 to at least the named place of destination.

The seller must provide the buyer with the insurance policy or other evidence of insurance cover.

Moreover, the seller must provide the buyer, at the buyer's request, risk, and expense (if any), with information that the buyer needs to procure any additional insurance.

A4. Delivery

The seller must deliver the goods by handing them over to the carrier contracted in accordance with A3 on the agreed date or within the agreed period.

A5. Transfer of risks

The seller bears all risks of loss of or damage to the goods until they have been delivered in accordance with A4, with the exception of loss or damage in the circumstances described in B5.

A6. Allocation of costs

The seller must pay

a) all costs relating to the goods until they have been delivered in accordance with A4, other than those payable by the buyer as envisaged in B6;

b) the freight and all other costs resulting from A3 a), including the costs of loading the goods and any charges for unloading at the place of destination that were for the seller's account under the contract of carriage;

c) the costs of insurance resulting from A3 b); and

d) where applicable, the costs of customs formalities necessary for export, as well as all duties, taxes and other charges payable upon export, and the costs for their transport through any country that were for the seller's account under the contract of carriage.

A7. Notices to the buyer

The seller must notify the buyer that the goods have been delivered in accordance with A4.

The seller must give the buyer any notice needed in order to allow the buyer to take measures that are normally necessary to enable the buyer to take the goods.

A8. Delivery document

If customary or at the buyer's request, the seller must provide the buyer, at the seller's expense, with the usual transport document [s] for the transport contracted in accordance with A3.

This transport document must cover the contract goods and be dated within the period agreed for shipment. If agreed or customary, the document must also enable the buyer to claim the goods from the carrier at the named place of destination and enable the buyer to sell the goods in transit by the transfer of the document to a subsequent buyer or by notification to the carrier.

When such a transport document is issued in negotiable form and in several originals, a full set of originals must be presented to the buyer.

A9. Checking – packaging – marking

The seller must pay the costs of those checking operations (such as checking quality, measuring, weighing, counting) that are necessary for the purpose of delivering the goods in accordance with A4 as well as the costs of any pre-shipment inspection mandated by the authority of the country of export. The seller must, at its own expense, package the goods, unless it is usual for the particular trade to transport the type of goods sold unpackaged.

The seller may package the goods in the manner appropriate for their transport, unless the buyer has notified the seller of specific packaging requirements before the contract of sale is concluded. Packaging is to be marked appropriately.

A10. Assistance with information and related costs

The seller must, where applicable, in a timely manner, provide to or render assistance in obtaining for the buyer, at the buyer's request, risk and expense, any documents and information, including security-related information, that the buyer needs for the import of the goods and/or for their transport to the final destination.

The seller must reimburse the buyer for all costs and charges incurred by the buyer in providing or rendering assistance in obtaining documents and information as envisaged in B10.

B. THE BUYER'S OBLIGATIONS

B1. General obligations of the buyer

The buyer must pay the price of the goods as provided in the contract of sale.

Any document referred to in B1 – B10 may be an equivalent electronic record or procedure if agreed between the parties or customary.

B2. Licences, authorizations, security clearances and other Formalities

Where applicable, it is up to the buyer to obtain, at its own risk and expense, any import licence or other official authorization and carry out all customs formalities for the import of the goods and for their transport through any country.

B3. Contracts of carriage and insurance

a) Contract of carriage

The buyer has no obligation to the seller to make a contract of carriage.

b) Contract of insurance

The buyer has no obligation to the seller to make a contract of insurance. However, the buyer must provide the seller, upon request, with any information necessary for the seller to procure any additional insurance requested by the buyer as envisaged in A3 b).

B4. Taking delivery

The buyer must take delivery of the goods when they have been delivered as envisaged in A4 and receive them from the carrier at the named place of destination.

B5. Transfer of risks

The buyer bears all risks of loss of or damage to the goods from the time they have been delivered as envisaged in A4.

If the buyer fails to give notice in accordance with B7, it must bear all risks of loss of or damage to the goods from the agreed date or the expiry date of the agreed period for delivery, provided that the goods have been clearly identified as the contract goods.

B6. Allocation of costs

The buyer must, subject to the provisions of A3 a), pay

a) all costs relating to the goods from the time they have been delivered as envisaged in A4, except, where applicable, the costs of customs formalities necessary for export, as well as all duties, taxes and other charges payable upon export as referred to in A6 d);

b) all costs and charges relating to the goods while in transit until their arrival at the agreed place of destination, unless such costs and charges were for the seller's account under the contract of carriage;

c) unloading costs, unless such costs were for the seller's account under the contract of carriage;

d) any additional costs incurred if it fails to give notice in accordance with B7, from the agreed date or the expiry date of the agreed period for dispatch, provided that the goods have been clearly identified as the contract goods;

e) where applicable, all duties, taxes and other charges as well as the costs of carrying out customs formalities payable upon import of the goods and the costs for their transport through any country, unless included within the cost of the contract of carriage; and

f) the costs of any additional insurance procured at the buyer's request under A3 and B3.

B7. Notices to the seller

The buyer must, whenever it is entitled to determine the time for dispatching the goods and/or the named place of destination or the point of receiving the goods within that place, give the seller sufficient notice thereof.

B8. Proof of delivery

The buyer must accept the transport document provided as envisaged in A8 if it is in conformity with the contract.

B9. Inspection of goods

The buyer must pay the costs of any mandatory pre-shipment inspection, except when such inspection is mandated by the authorities of the country of export.

B10. Assistance with information and related costs

The buyer must, in a timely manner, advise the seller of any security information requirements so that the seller may comply with A10.

The buyer must reimburse the seller for all costs and charges incurred by the seller in providing or rendering assistance in obtaining documents and information as envisaged in A10.

The buyer must, where applicable, in a timely manner, provide to or render assistance in obtaining for the seller, at the seller's request, risk and expense, any documents and information, including security-related information, that the seller needs for the transport and export of the goods and for their transport through any country.

3.2.5 DAT—Delivered at Terminal

This rule may be used irrespective of the mode of transport selected and may also be used where more than one mode of transport is employed.

"Delivered at Terminal" means that the seller delivers when the goods, once unloaded from the arriving means of transport, are placed at the disposal of the buyer at a named terminal at the named port or place of destination. "Terminal" includes any place, whether covered or not, such as a quay, warehouse, container yard or road, rail or air cargo terminal. The seller bears all risks involved in bringing the goods to and unloading them at the terminal at the named port or place of destination.

The parties are well advised to specify as clearly as possible the terminal and, if possible, a specific point within the terminal at the agreed port or place of destination, as the risks to that point are for the account of the seller. The seller is advised to procure a contract of carriage that matches this choice precisely.

Moreover, if the parties intend the seller to bear the risks and costs involved in transporting and handling the goods from the terminal to another place, then the DAP or DDP rules should be used.

DAT requires the seller to clear the goods for export, where applicable. However, the seller has no obligation to clear the goods for import, pay any import duty or carry out any import customs formalities.

A. THE SELLER'S OBLIGATIONS

A1. General obligations of the seller

The seller must provide the goods and the commercial invoice in conformity with the contract of sale and any other evidence of conformity that may be required by the contract.

Any document referred to in A1 – A10 may be an equivalent electronic record or procedure if agreed between the parties or customary.

A2. Licences, authorizations, security clearances and other formalities

Where applicable, the seller must obtain, at its own risk and expense, any export licence and other official authorization and carry out all customs formalities necessary for the export of the goods and for their transport through any country prior to delivery.

A3. Contracts of carriage and insurance

a) Contract of carriage

The seller must contract at its own expense for the carriage of the goods to the named terminal at the agreed port or place of destination. If a specific terminal is not agreed or is not determined by practice, the seller may select the terminal at the agreed port or place of destination that best suits its purpose.

b) Contract of insurance

The seller has no obligation to the buyer to make a contract of insurance. However, the seller must provide the buyer, at the buyer's request, risk, and expense (if any), with information that the buyer needs for obtaining insurance.

A4. Delivery

The seller must unload the goods from the arriving means of transport and must then deliver them by placing them at the disposal of the buyer at the named terminal referred to in A3 a) at the port or place of destination on the agreed date or within the agreed period.

A5. Transfer of risks

The seller bears all risks of loss of or damage to the goods until they have been delivered in accordance with A4 with the exception of loss or damage in the circumstances described in B5.

A6. Allocation of costs

The seller must pay

a) in addition to costs resulting from A3 a), all costs relating to the goods until they have been delivered in accordance with A4, other than those payable by the buyer as envisaged in B6; and

b) where applicable, the costs of customs formalities necessary for export as well as all duties, taxes and other charges payable upon export and the costs for their transport through any country, prior to delivery in accordance with A4.

A7. Notices to the buyer

The seller must give the buyer any notice needed in order to allow the buyer to take measures that are normally necessary to enable the buyer to take delivery of the goods.

A8. Delivery document

The seller must provide the buyer, at the seller's expense, with a document enabling the buyer to take delivery of the goods as envisaged in A4/B4.

A9. Checking – packaging – marking

The seller must pay the costs of those checking operations (such as checking quality, measuring, weighing, counting) that are necessary for the purpose of delivering the goods in accordance with A4, as well as the costs of any pre-shipment inspection mandated by the authority of the country of export.

The seller must, at its own expense, package the goods, unless it is usual for the particular trade to transport the type of goods sold unpackaged. The seller may package the goods in the manner appropriate for their transport, unless the buyer has notified the seller of specific packaging requirements before the contract of sale is concluded. Packaging is to be marked appropriately.

A10. Assistance with information and related costs

The seller must, where applicable, in a timely manner, provide to or render assistance in obtaining for the buyer, at the buyer's request, risk and expense, any documents and information, including security-related information, that the buyer needs for the import of the goods and/or for their transport to the final destination.

The seller must reimburse the buyer for all costs and charges incurred by the buyer in providing or rendering assistance in obtaining documents and information as envisaged in B10.

B. THE BUYER'S OBLIGATIONS

B1. General obligations of the buyer

The buyer must pay the price of the goods as provided in the contract of sale.

Any document referred to in B1 – B10 may be an equivalent electronic record or procedure if agreed between the parties or customary.

B2. Licences, authorizations, security clearances and other formalities

Where applicable, the buyer must obtain, at its own risk and expense, any import licence or other official authorization and carry out all customs formalities for the import of the goods.

B3. Contracts of carriage and insurance

a) Contract of carriage

The buyer has no obligation to the seller to make a contract of carriage.

b) Contract of insurance

The buyer has no obligation to the seller to make a contract of insurance. However, the buyer must provide the seller, upon request, with the necessary information for obtaining insurance.

B4. Taking delivery

The buyer must take delivery of the goods when they have been delivered as envisaged in A4.

B5. Transfer of risks

The buyer bears all risks of loss of or damage to the goods from the time they have been delivered as envisaged in A4.

If

a) the buyer fails to fulfill its obligations in accordance with B2, then it bears all resulting risks of loss of or damage to the goods; or

b) the buyer fails to give notice in accordance with B7, then it bears all risks of loss of or damage to the goods from the agreed date or the expiry date of the agreed period for delivery,

provided that the goods have been clearly identified as the contract goods.

B6. Allocation of costs

The buyer must pay

a) all costs relating to the goods from the time they have been delivered as envisaged in A4;

b) any additional costs incurred by the seller if the buyer fails to fulfill its obligations in accordance with B2, or to give notice in accordance with B7, provided that the goods have been clearly identified as the contract goods; and

c) where applicable, the costs of customs formalities as well as all duties, taxes and other charges payable upon import of the goods.

B7. Notices to the seller

The buyer must, whenever it is entitled to determine the time within an agreed period and/or the point of taking delivery at the named terminal, give the seller sufficient notice thereof.

B8. Proof of delivery

The buyer must accept the delivery document provided as envisaged in A8.

B9. Inspection of goods

The buyer must pay the costs of any mandatory pre-shipment inspection, except when such inspection is mandated by the authorities of the country of export.

B10. Assistance with information and related costs

The buyer must, in a timely manner, advise the seller of any security information requirements so that the seller may comply with A10.

The buyer must reimburse the seller for all costs and charges incurred by the seller in providing or rendering assistance in obtaining documents and information as envisaged in A10.

The buyer must, where applicable, in a timely manner, provide to or render assistance in obtaining for the seller, at the seller's request, risk and expense, any documents and information, including security-related information, that the seller needs for the transport and export of the goods and for their transport through any country.

3.2.6 DAP—Delivered at Place

This rule may be used irrespective of the mode of transport selected and may also be used where more than one mode of transport is employed.

"Delivered at Place" means that the seller delivers when the goods are placed at the disposal of the buyer on the arriving means of transport ready for unloading at the named place of destination. The seller bears all risks involved in bringing the goods to the named place.

The parties are well advised to specify as clearly as possible the point within the agreed place of destination, as the risks to that point are for the account of the seller. The seller is advised to procure contracts of carriage that match this choice precisely. If the seller incurs costs under its contract of carriage related to unloading at the place of destination, the seller is not entitled to recover such costs from the buyer unless otherwise agreed between the parties.

DAP requires the seller to clear the goods for export, where applicable. However, the seller has no obligation to clear the goods for import, pay any import duty or carry out any import customs formalities. If the parties wish the seller to clear the goods for import, pay any import duty and carry out any import customs formalities, the DDP term should be used.

A. THE SELLER'S OBLIGATIONS

A1. General obligations of the seller

The seller must provide the goods and the commercial invoice in conformity with the contract of sale and any other evidence of conformity that may be required by the contract.

Any document referred to in A1 – A10 may be an equivalent electronic record or procedure if agreed between the parties or customary.

A2. Licences, authorizations, security clearances and other formalities

Where applicable, the seller must obtain, at its own risk and expense, any export licence and other official authorization and carry out all customs formalities necessary for the export of the goods and for their transport through any country prior to delivery.

A3. Contracts of carriage and insurance

a) Contract of carriage

The seller must contract at its own expense for the carriage of the goods to the named place of destination or to the agreed point, if any, at the named place of destination. If a specific point is not agreed or is not determined by practice, the seller may select the point at the named place of destination that best suits its purpose.

b) Contract of insurance

The seller has no obligation to the buyer to make a contract of insurance. However, the seller must provide the buyer, at the buyer's request, risk, and expense (if any), with information that the buyer needs for obtaining insurance.

A4. Delivery

The seller must deliver the goods by placing them at the disposal of the buyer on the arriving means of transport ready for unloading at the agreed point, if any, at the named place of destination on the agreed date or within the agreed period.

A5. Transfer of risks

The seller bears all risks of loss of or damage to the goods until they have been delivered in accordance with A4, with the exception of loss or damage in the circumstances described in B5.

A6. Allocation of costs

The seller must pay

a) in addition to costs resulting from A3 a), all costs relating to the goods until they have been delivered in accordance with A4, other than those payable by the buyer as envisaged in B6;

b) any charges for unloading at the place of destination that were for the seller's account under the contract of carriage; and

c) where applicable, the costs of customs formalities necessary for export as well as all duties, taxes and other charges payable upon export and the costs for their transport through any country, prior to delivery in accordance with A4.

A7. Notices to the buyer

The seller must give the buyer any notice needed in order to allow the buyer to take measures that are normally necessary to enable the buyer to take delivery of the goods.

A8. Delivery document

The seller must provide the buyer, at the seller's expense, with a document enabling the buyer to take delivery of the goods as envisaged in A4/B4.

A9. Checking – packaging – marking

The seller must pay the costs of those checking operations (such as checking quality, measuring, weighing, counting) that are necessary for the purpose of delivering the goods in accordance with A4, as well as the costs of any pre-shipment inspection mandated by the authority of the country of export.

The seller must, at its own expense, package the goods, unless it is usual for the particular trade to transport the type of goods sold unpackaged. The seller may package the goods in the manner appropriate for their transport, unless the buyer has notified the seller of specific packaging requirements before the contract of sale is concluded. Packaging is to be marked appropriately.

A10. Assistance with information and related costs

The seller must, where applicable, in a timely manner, provide to or render assistance in obtaining for the buyer, at the buyer's request, risk and expense, any documents and information, including security-related information, that the buyer needs for the import of the goods and/or for their transport to the final destination.

The seller must reimburse the buyer for all costs and charges incurred by the buyer in providing or rendering assistance in obtaining documents and information as envisaged in B10.

B. THE BUYER'S OBLIGATIONS

B1. General obligations of the buyer

The buyer must pay the price of the goods as provided in the contract of sale.

Any document referred to in B1 – B10 may be an equivalent electronic record or procedure if agreed between the parties or customary.

B2. Licences, authorizations, security clearances and other formalities

Where applicable, the buyer must obtain, at its own risk and expense, any import licence or other official authorization and carry out all customs formalities for the import of the goods.

B3. Contracts of carriage and insurance

a) Contract of carriage

The buyer has no obligation to the seller to make a contract of carriage.

b) Contract of insurance

The buyer has no obligation to the seller to make a contract of insurance. However, the buyer must provide the seller, upon request, with the necessary information for obtaining insurance.

B4. Taking delivery

The buyer must take delivery of the goods when they have been delivered as envisaged in A4.

B5. Transfer of risks

The buyer bears all risks of loss of or damage to the goods from the time they have been delivered as envisaged in A4.

If

a) the buyer fails to fulfill its obligations in accordance with B2, then it bears all resulting risks of loss of or damage to the goods; or

b) the buyer fails to give notice in accordance with B7, then it bears all risks of loss of or damage to the goods from the agreed date or the expiry date of the agreed period for delivery,

provided that the goods have been clearly identified as the contract goods.

B6. Allocation of costs

The buyer must pay

a) all costs relating to the goods from the time they have been delivered as envisaged in A4;

b) all costs of unloading necessary to take delivery of the goods from the arriving means of transport at the named place of destination, unless such costs were for the seller's account under the contract of carriage;

c) any additional costs incurred by the seller if the buyer fails to fulfill its obligations in accordance with B2 or to give notice in accordance with B7, provided that the goods have been clearly identified as the contract goods; and

d) where applicable, the costs of customs formalities, as well as all duties, taxes and other charges payable upon import of the goods.

B7. Notices to the seller

The buyer must, whenever it is entitled to determine the time within an agreed period and/or the point of taking delivery within the named place of destination, give the seller sufficient notice thereof.

B8. Proof of delivery

The buyer must accept the delivery document provided as envisaged in A8.

B9. Inspection of goods

The buyer must pay the costs of any mandatory pre-shipment inspection, except when such inspection is mandated by the authorities of the country of export.

B10. Assistance with information and related costs

The buyer must, in a timely manner, advise the seller of any security information requirements so that the seller may comply with A10.

The buyer must reimburse the seller for all costs and charges incurred by the seller in providing or rendering assistance in obtaining documents and information as envisaged in A10.

The buyer must, where applicable, in a timely manner, provide to or render assistance in obtaining for the seller, at the seller's request, risk and expense, any documents and information, including security-related information, that the seller needs for the transport and export of the goods and for their transport through any country.

3.2.7 DDP—Delivered Duty Paid

This rule may be used irrespective of the mode of transport selected and may also be used where more than one mode of transport is employed.

"Delivered Duty Paid" means that the seller delivers the goods when the goods are placed at the disposal of the buyer, cleared for import on the arriving means of transport ready for unloading at the named place of destination. The seller bears all the costs and risks involved in bringing the goods to the place of destination and has an obligation to clear the goods not only for export but also for import, to pay any duty for both export and import and to carry out all customs formalities.

DDP represents the maximum obligation for the seller. The parties are well advised to specify as clearly as possible the point within the agreed place of destination, as the costs and risks to that point are for the account of the seller. The seller is advised to procure contracts of carriage that match this choice precisely. If the seller incurs costs under its contract of carriage related to unloading at the place of destination, the seller is not entitled to recover such costs from the buyer unless otherwise agreed between the parties.

The parties are well advised not to use DDP if the seller is unable directly or indirectly to obtain import clearance.

If the parties wish the buyer to bear all risks and costs of import clearance, the DAP rule should be used.

Any VAT or other taxes payable upon import are for the seller's account unless expressly agreed otherwise in the sales contract.

A. THE SELLER'S OBLIGATIONS

A1. General obligations of the seller

The seller must provide the goods and the commercial invoice in conformity with the contract of sale and any other evidence of conformity that may be required by the contract.

Any document referred to in A1 – A10 may be an equivalent electronic record or procedure if agreed between the parties or customary.

A2. Licences, authorizations, security clearances and other formalities

Where applicable, the seller must obtain, at its own risk and expense, any export and import licence and other official authorization and carry out all customs formalities necessary for the export of the goods, for their transport through any country and for their import.

A3. Contracts of carriage and insurance

a) Contract of carriage

The seller must contract at its own expense for the carriage of the goods to the named place of destination or to the agreed point, if any, at the named place of destination. If a specific point is not agreed or is not determined by practice, the seller may select the point at the named place of destination that best suits its purpose.

b) Contract of insurance

The seller has no obligation to the buyer to make a contract of insurance. However, the seller must provide the buyer, at the buyer's request, risk, and expense (if any), with information that the buyer needs for obtaining insurance.

A4. Delivery

The seller must deliver the goods by placing them at the disposal of the buyer on the arriving means of transport ready for unloading at the agreed point, if any, at the named place of destination on the agreed date or within the agreed period.

A5. Transfer of risks

The seller bears all risks of loss of or damage to the goods until they have been delivered in accordance with A4, with the exception of loss or damage in the circumstances described in B5.

A6. Allocation of costs

The seller must pay

a) in addition to costs resulting from A3 a), all costs relating to the goods until they have been delivered in accordance with A4, other than those payable by the buyer as envisaged in B6;

b) any charges for unloading at the place of destination that were for the seller's account under the contract of carriage; and

c) where applicable, the costs of customs formalities necessary for export and import as well as all duties, taxes and other charges payable upon export and import of the goods, and the costs for their transport through any country prior to delivery in accordance with A4.

A7. Notices to the buyer

The seller must give the buyer any notice needed in order to allow the buyer to take measures that are normally necessary to enable the buyer to take delivery of the goods.

A8. Delivery document

The seller must provide the buyer, at the seller's expense, with a document enabling the buyer to take delivery of the goods as envisaged in A4/B4.

A9. Checking – packaging – marking

The seller must pay the costs of those checking operations (such as checking quality, measuring, weighing, counting) that are necessary for the purpose of delivering the goods in accordance with A4, as well as the costs of any pre-shipment inspection mandated by the authority of the country of export or of import.

The seller must, at its own expense, package the goods, unless it is usual for the particular trade to transport the type of goods sold unpackaged. The seller may package the goods in the manner appropriate for their transport, unless the buyer has notified the seller of specific packaging requirements before the contract of sale is concluded. Packaging is to be marked appropriately.

A10. Assistance with information and related costs

The seller must, where applicable, in a timely manner, provide to or render assistance in obtaining for the buyer, at the buyer's request, risk and expense, any documents and information, including security-related information, that the buyer needs for the transport of the goods to the final destination, where applicable, from the named place of destination.

The seller must reimburse the buyer for all costs and charges incurred by the buyer in providing or rendering assistance in obtaining documents and information as envisaged in B10.

B. THE BUYER'S OBLIGATIONS

B1. General obligations of the buyer

The buyer must pay the price of the goods as provided in the contract of sale.

Any document referred to in B1 – B10 may be an equivalent electronic record or procedure if agreed between the parties or customary.

B2. Licences, authorizations, security clearances and other formalities

Where applicable, the buyer must provide assistance to the seller, at the seller's request, risk and expense, in obtaining any import licence or other official authorization for the import of the goods.

B3. Contracts of carriage and insurance

a) Contract of carriage

The buyer has no obligation to the seller to make a contract of carriage.

b) Contract of insurance

The buyer has no obligation to the seller to make a contract of insurance. However, the buyer must provide the seller, upon request, with the necessary information for obtaining insurance.

B4. Taking delivery

The buyer must take delivery of the goods when they have been delivered as envisaged in A4.

B5. Transfer of risks

The buyer bears all risks of loss of or damage to the goods from the time they have been delivered as envisaged in A4.

If

a) the buyer fails to fulfill its obligations in accordance with B2, then it bears all resulting risks of loss of or damage to the goods; or

b) the buyer fails to give notice in accordance with B7, then it bears all risks of loss of or damage to the goods from the agreed date or the expiry date of the agreed period for delivery, provided that the goods have been clearly identified as the contract goods.

B6. Allocation of costs

The buyer must pay

a) all costs relating to the goods from the time they have been delivered as envisaged in A4;

b) all costs of unloading necessary to take delivery of the goods from the arriving means of transport at the named place of destination, unless such costs were for the seller's account under the contract of carriage; and

c) any additional costs incurred if it fails to fulfill its obligations in accordance with B2 or to give notice in accordance with B7, provided that the goods have been clearly identified as the contract goods.

B7. Notices to the seller

The buyer must, whenever it is entitled to determine the time within an agreed period and/or the point of taking delivery within the named place of destination, give the seller sufficient notice thereof.

B8. Proof of delivery

The buyer must accept the proof of delivery provided as envisaged in A8.

B9. Inspection of goods

The buyer has no obligation to the seller to pay the costs of any mandatory pre-shipment inspection mandated by the authority of the country of export or of import.

B10. Assistance with information and related costs

The buyer must, in a timely manner, advise the seller of any security information requirements so that the seller may comply with A10.

The buyer must reimburse the seller for all costs and charges incurred by the seller in providing or rendering assistance in obtaining documents and information as envisaged in A10.

The buyer must, where applicable, in a timely manner, provide to or render assistance in obtaining for the seller, at the seller's request, risk and expense, any documents and information, including security-related information, that the seller needs for the transport, export and import of the goods and for their transport through any country.

3.2.8 FAS—Free Alongside Ship

This rule is to be used only for sea or inland waterway transport.

"Free Alongside Ship" means that the seller delivers when the goods are placed alongside the vessel (e.g., on a quay or a barge) nominated by the buyer at the named port of shipment. The risk of loss of or damage to the goods passes when the goods are alongside the ship, and the buyer bears all costs from that moment onwards.

The parties are well advised to specify as clearly as possible the loading point at the named port of shipment, as the costs and risks to that point are for the account of the seller and these costs and associated handling charges may vary according to the practice of the port.

The seller is required either to deliver the goods alongside the ship or to procure goods already so delivered for shipment. The reference to "procure" here caters for multiple sales down a chain ("string sales"), particularly common in the commodity trades.

Where the goods are in containers, it is typical for the seller to hand the goods over to the carrier at a terminal and not alongside the vessel. In such situations, the FAS rule would be inappropriate, and the FCA rule should be used.

FAS requires the seller to clear the goods for export, where applicable. However, the seller has no obligation to clear the goods for import, pay any import duty or carry out any import customs formalities.

A. THE SELLER'S OBLIGATIONS

A1. General obligations of the seller

The seller must provide the goods and the commercial invoice in conformity with the contract of sale and any other evidence of conformity that may be required by the contract.

Any document referred to in A1 – A10 may be an equivalent electronic record or procedure if agreed between the parties or customary.

A2. Licences, authorizations, security clearances and other formalities

Where applicable, the seller must obtain, at its own risk and expense, any export licence or other official authorization and carry out all customs formalities necessary for the export of the goods.

A3. Contracts of carriage and insurance

a) Contract of carriage

The seller has no obligation to the buyer to make a contract of carriage. However, if requested by the buyer or if it is commercial practice and the buyer does not give an instruction to the contrary in due time, the seller may contract for carriage on usual terms at the buyer's risk and expense. In either case, the seller may decline to make the contract of carriage and, if it does, shall promptly notify the buyer.

b) Contract of insurance

The seller has no obligation to the buyer to make a contract of insurance. However, the seller must provide the buyer, at the buyer's request, risk, and expense (if any), with information that the buyer needs for obtaining insurance.

A4. Delivery

The seller must deliver the goods either by placing them alongside the ship nominated by the buyer at the loading point, if any, indicated by the buyer at the named port of shipment or by procuring the goods so delivered. In either case, the seller must deliver the goods on the agreed date or within the agreed period and in the manner customary at the port.

If no specific loading point has been indicated by the buyer, the seller may select the point within the named port of shipment that best suits its purpose. If the parties have agreed that delivery should take place within a period, the buyer has the option to choose the date within that period.

A5. Transfer of risks

The seller bears all risks of loss of or damage to the goods until they have been delivered in accordance with A4 with the exception of loss or damage in the circumstances described in B5.

A6. Allocation of costs

The seller must pay

a) all costs relating to the goods until they have been delivered in accordance with A4, other than those payable by the buyer as envisaged in B6; and

b) where applicable, the costs of customs formalities necessary for export as well as all duties, taxes and other charges payable upon export.

A7. Notices to the buyer

The seller must, at the buyer's risk and expense, give the buyer sufficient notice either that the goods have been delivered in accordance with A4 or that the vessel has failed to take the goods within the time agreed.

A8. Delivery document

The seller must provide the buyer, at the seller's expense, with the usual proof that the goods have been delivered in accordance with A4.

Unless such proof is a transport document, the seller must provide assistance to the buyer, at the buyer's request, risk and expense, in obtaining a transport document.

A9. Checking – packaging – marking

The seller must pay the costs of those checking operations (such as checking quality, measuring, weighing, counting) that are necessary for the purpose of delivering the goods in accordance with A4, as well as the costs of any pre-shipment inspection mandated by the authority of the country of export.

The seller must, at its own expense, package the goods, unless it is usual for the particular trade to transport the type of goods sold unpackaged. The seller may package the goods in the manner appropriate for their transport, unless the buyer has notified the seller of specific packaging requirements before the contract of sale is concluded. Packaging is to be marked appropriately.

A10. Assistance with information and related costs

The seller must, where applicable, in a timely manner, provide to or render assistance in obtaining for the buyer, at the buyer's request, risk and expense, any documents and information, including security-related information, that the buyer needs for the import of the goods and/or for their transport to the final destination.

The seller must reimburse the buyer for all costs and charges incurred by the buyer in providing or rendering assistance in obtaining documents and information as envisaged in B10.

B. THE BUYER'S OBLIGATIONS

B1. General obligations of the buyer

The buyer must pay the price of the goods as provided in the contract of sale.

Any document referred to in B1 – B10 may be an equivalent electronic record or procedure if agreed between the parties or customary.

B2. Licences, authorizations, security clearances and other formalities

Where applicable, it is up to the buyer to obtain, at its own risk and expense, any import licence or other official authorization and carry out all customs formalities for the import of the goods and for their transport through any country.

B3. Contracts of carriage and insurance

a) Contract of carriage

The buyer must contract, at its own expense for the carriage of the goods from the named port of shipment, except where the contract of carriage is made by the seller as provided for in A3 a).

b) Contract of insurance

The buyer has no obligation to the seller to make a contract of insurance.

B4. Taking delivery

The buyer must take delivery of the goods when they have been delivered as envisaged in A4.

B5. Transfer of risks

The buyer bears all risks of loss of or damage to the goods from the time they have been delivered as envisaged in A4.

If

a) the buyer fails to give notice in accordance with B7; or

b) the vessel nominated by the buyer fails to arrive on time, or fails to take the goods or closes for cargo earlier than the time notified in accordance with B7;

then the buyer bears all risks of loss of or damage to the goods from the agreed date or the expiry date of the agreed period for delivery, provided that the goods have been clearly identified as the contract goods.

B6. Allocation of costs

The buyer must pay

a) all costs relating to the goods from the time they have been delivered as envisaged in A4, except, where applicable, the costs of customs formalities necessary for export as well as all duties, taxes, and other charges payable upon export as referred to in A6 b);

b) any additional costs incurred, either because:

(i) the buyer has failed to give appropriate notice in accordance with B7, or

(ii) the vessel nominated by the buyer fails to arrive on time, is unable to take the goods, or closes for cargo earlier than the time notified in accordance with B7,

provided that the goods have been clearly identified as the contract goods; and

c) where applicable, all duties, taxes and other charges, as well as the costs of carrying out customs formalities payable upon import of the goods and the costs for their transport through any country.

B7. Notices to the seller

The buyer must give the seller sufficient notice of the vessel name, loading point and, where necessary, the selected delivery time within the agreed period.

B8. Proof of delivery

The buyer must accept the proof of delivery provided as envisaged in A8.

B9. Inspection of goods

The buyer must pay the costs of any mandatory pre-shipment inspection, except when such inspection is mandated by the authorities of the country of export.

B10. Assistance with information and related costs

The buyer must, in a timely manner, advise the seller of any security information requirements so that the seller may comply with A10.

The buyer must reimburse the seller for all costs and charges incurred by the seller in providing or rendering assistance in obtaining documents and information as envisaged in A10.

The buyer must, where applicable, in a timely manner, provide to or render assistance in obtaining for the seller, at the seller's request, risk and expense, any documents and information, including security-related information, that the seller needs for the transport and export of the goods and for their transport through any country.

3.2.9 FOB—Free on Board

This rule is to be used only for sea or inland waterway transport.

"Free on Board" means that the seller delivers the goods on board the vessel nominated by the buyer at the named port of shipment or procures the goods already so delivered. The risk of loss of or damage to the goods passes when the goods are on board the vessel, and the buyer bears all costs from that moment onwards.

The seller is required either to deliver the goods on board the vessel or to procure goods already so delivered for shipment. The reference to "procure" here caters for multiple sales down a chain ("string sales"), particularly common in the commodity trades.

FOB may not be appropriate where goods are handed over to the carrier before they are on board the vessel, for example goods in containers, which are typically delivered at a terminal. In such situations, the FCA rule should be used.

FOB requires the seller to clear the goods for export, where applicable. However, the seller has no obligation to clear the goods for import, pay any import duty or carry out any import customs formalities.

A. THE SELLER'S OBLIGATIONS

A1. General obligations of the seller

The seller must provide the goods and the commercial invoice in conformity with the contract of sale and any other evidence of conformity that may be required by the contract.

Any document referred to in A1 – A10 may be an equivalent electronic record or procedure if agreed between the parties or customary.

A2. Licences, authorizations, security clearances and other formalities

Where applicable, the seller must obtain, at its own risk and expense, any export licence or other official authorization and carry out all customs formalities necessary for the export of the goods.

A3. Contracts of carriage and insurance

a) Contract of carriage

The seller has no obligation to the buyer to make a contract of carriage. However, if requested by the buyer or if it is commercial practice and the buyer does not give an instruction to the contrary in due time, the seller may contract for carriage on usual terms at the buyer's risk and expense. In either case, the seller may decline to make the contract of carriage and, if it does, shall promptly notify the buyer.

b) Contract of insurance

The seller has no obligation to the buyer to make a contract of insurance. However, the seller must provide the buyer, at the buyer's request, risk, and expense (if any), with information that the buyer needs for obtaining insurance.

A4. Delivery

The seller must deliver the goods either by placing them on board the vessel nominated by the buyer at the loading point, if any, indicated by the buyer at the named port of shipment or by procuring the goods so delivered. In either case, the seller must deliver the goods on the agreed date or within the agreed period and in the manner customary at the port.

If no specific loading point has been indicated by the buyer, the seller may select the point within the named port of shipment that best suits its purpose.

A5. Transfer of risks

The seller bears all risks of loss of or damage to the goods until they have been delivered in accordance with A4 with the exception of loss or damage in the circumstances described in B5.

A6. Allocation of costs

The seller must pay

a) all costs relating to the goods until they have been delivered in accordance with A4, other than those payable by the buyer as envisaged in B6; and

b) where applicable, the costs of customs formalities necessary for export, as well as all duties, taxes and other charges payable upon export.

A7. Notices to the buyer

The seller must, at the buyer's risk and expense, give the buyer sufficient notice either that the goods have been delivered in accordance with A4 or that the vessel has failed to take the goods within the time agreed.

A8. Delivery document

The seller must provide the buyer, at the seller's expense, with the usual proof that the goods have been delivered in accordance with A4.

Unless such proof is a transport document, the seller must provide assistance to the buyer, at the buyer's request, risk and expense, in obtaining a transport document.

A9. Checking – packaging – marking

The seller must pay the costs of those checking operations (such as checking quality, measuring, weighing, counting) that are necessary for the purpose of delivering the goods in accordance with A4, as well as the costs of any pre-shipment inspection mandated by the authority of the country of export.

The seller must, at its own expense, package the goods, unless it is usual for the particular trade to transport the type of goods sold unpackaged. The seller may package the goods in the manner appropriate for their transport, unless the buyer has notified the seller of specific packaging requirements before the contract of sale is concluded. Packaging is to be marked appropriately.

A10. Assistance with information and related costs

The seller must, where applicable, in a timely manner, provide to or render assistance in obtaining for the buyer, at the buyer's request, risk and expense, any documents and information, including security-related information, that the buyer needs for the import of the goods and/or for their transport to the final destination.

The seller must reimburse the buyer for all costs and charges incurred by the buyer in providing or rendering assistance in obtaining documents and information as envisaged in B10.

B. THE BUYER'S OBLIGATIONS

B1. General obligations of the buyer

The buyer must pay the price of the goods as provided in the contract of sale.

Any document referred to in B1 – B10 may be an equivalent electronic record or procedure if agreed between the parties or customary.

B2. Licences, authorizations, security clearances and other formalities

Where applicable, it is up to the buyer to obtain, at its own risk and expense, any import licence or other official authorization and carry out all customs formalities for the import of the goods and for their transport through any country.

B3. Contracts of carriage and insurance

a) Contract of carriage

The buyer must contract, at its own expense for the carriage of the goods from the named port of shipment, except where the contract of carriage is made by the seller as provided for in A3 a).

b) Contract of insurance

The buyer has no obligation to the seller to make a contract of insurance.

B4. Taking delivery

The buyer must take delivery of the goods when they have been delivered as envisaged in A4.

B5. Transfer of risks

The buyer bears all risks of loss of or damage to the goods from the time they have been delivered as envisaged in A4.

If

a) the buyer fails to notify the nomination of a vessel in accordance with B7; or

b) the vessel nominated by the buyer fails to arrive on time to enable the seller to comply with A4, is unable to take the goods, or closes for cargo earlier than the time notified in accordance with B7; then, the buyer bears all risks of loss of or damage to the goods:

(i) from the agreed date, or in the absence of an agreed date,

(ii) from the date notified by the seller under A7 within the agreed period, or, if no such date has been notified,

(iii) from the expiry date of any agreed period for delivery, provided that the goods have been clearly identified as the contract goods.

B6. Allocation of costs

The buyer must pay

a) all costs relating to the goods from the time they have been delivered as envisaged in A4, except, where applicable, the costs of customs formalities necessary for export, as well as all duties, taxes and other charges payable upon export as referred to in A6 b);

b) any additional costs incurred, either because:

(i) the buyer has failed to give appropriate notice in accordance with B7, or

(ii) the vessel nominated by the buyer fails to arrive on time, is unable to take the goods, or closes for cargo earlier than the time notified in accordance with B7, provided that the goods have been clearly identified as the contract goods; and

c) where applicable, all duties, taxes and other charges, as well as the costs of carrying out customs formalities payable upon import of the goods and the costs for their transport through any country.

B7. Notices to the seller

The buyer must give the seller sufficient notice of the vessel name, loading point and, where necessary, the selected delivery time within the agreed period.

B8. Proof of delivery

The buyer must accept the proof of delivery provided as envisaged in A8.

B9. Inspection of goods

The buyer must pay the costs of any mandatory pre-shipment inspection, except when such inspection is mandated by the authorities of the country of export.

B10. Assistance with information and related costs

The buyer must, in a timely manner, advise the seller of any security information requirements so that the seller may comply with A10.

The buyer must reimburse the seller for all costs and charges incurred by the seller in providing or rendering assistance in obtaining documents and information as envisaged in A10.

The buyer must, where applicable, in a timely manner, provide to or render assistance in obtaining for the seller, at the seller's request, risk and expense, any documents and information, including security-related information, that the seller needs for the transport and export of the goods and for their transport through any country.

3.2.10 CFR—Cost and Freight

This rule is to be used only for sea or inland waterway transport.

"Cost and Freight" means that the seller delivers the goods on board the vessel or procures the goods already so delivered. The risk of loss of or damage to the goods passes when the goods are on board the vessel.

The seller must contract for and pay the costs and freight necessary to bring the goods to the named port of destination.

When CPT, CIP, CFR or CIF are used, the seller fulfils its obligation to deliver when it hands the goods over to the carrier in the manner specified in the chosen rule and not when the goods reach the place of destination.

This rule has two critical points, because risk passes and costs are transferred at different places. While the contract will always specify a destination port, it might not specify the port of shipment, which is where risk passes to the buyer. If the shipment port is of particular interest to the buyer, the parties are well advised to identify it as precisely as possible in the contract.

The parties are well advised to identify as precisely as possible the point at the agreed port of destination, as the costs to that point are for the account of the seller. The seller is advised to procure contracts of carriage that match this choice precisely. If the seller incurs costs under its contract of carriage related to unloading at the specified point at the port of destination, the seller is not entitled to recover such costs from the buyer unless otherwise agreed between the parties.

The seller is required either to deliver the goods on board the vessel or to procure goods already so delivered for shipment to the destination.

In addition, the seller is required either to make a contract of carriage or to procure such a contract. The reference to "procure" here caters for multiple sales down a chain ("string sales"), particularly common in the commodity trades.

CFR may not be appropriate where goods are handed over to the carrier before they are on board the vessel, for example goods in containers, which are typically delivered at a terminal. In such circumstances, the CPT rule should be used.

CFR requires the seller to clear the goods for export, where applicable. However, the seller has no obligation to clear the goods for import, pay any import duty or carry out any import customs formalities.

A. THE SELLER'S OBLIGATIONS

A1. General obligations of the seller

The seller must provide the goods and the commercial invoice in conformity with the contract of sale and any other evidence of conformity that may be required by the contract.

Any document referred to in A1 – A10 may be an equivalent electronic record or procedure if agreed between the parties or customary.

A2. Licences, authorizations, security clearances and other formalities

Where applicable, the seller must obtain, at its own risk and expense, any export licence or other official authorization and carry out all customs formalities necessary for the export of the goods.

A3. Contracts of carriage and insurance

a) Contract of carriage

The seller must contract or procure a contract for the carriage of the goods from the agreed point of delivery, if any, at the place of delivery to the named port of destination or, if agreed, any point at that port. The contract of carriage must be made on usual terms at the seller's expense and provide for carriage by the usual route in a vessel of the type normally used for the transport of the type of goods sold.

b) Contract of insurance

The seller has no obligation to the buyer to make a contract of insurance. However, the seller must provide the buyer, at the buyer's request, risk, and expense (if any), with information that the buyer needs for obtaining insurance.

A4. Delivery

The seller must deliver the goods either by placing them on board the vessel or by procuring the goods so delivered. In either case, the seller must deliver the goods on the agreed date or within the agreed period and in the manner customary at the port.

A5. Transfer of risks

The seller bears all risks of loss of or damage to the goods until they have been delivered in accordance with A4, with the exception of loss or damage in the circumstances described in B5.

A6. Allocation of costs

The seller must pay

a) all costs relating to the goods until they have been delivered in accordance with A4, other than those payable by the buyer as envisaged in B6;

b) the freight and all other costs resulting from A3 a), including the costs of loading the goods on board and any charges for unloading at the agreed port of discharge that were for the seller's account under the contract of carriage; and

c) where applicable, the costs of customs formalities necessary for export as well as all duties, taxes and other charges payable upon export, and the costs for their transport through any country that were for the seller's account under the contract of carriage.

A7. Notices to the buyer

The seller must give the buyer any notice needed in order to allow the buyer to take measures that are normally necessary to enable the buyer to take the goods.

A8. Delivery document

The seller must, at its own expense, provide the buyer without delay with the usual transport document for the agreed port of destination.

This transport document must cover the contract goods, be dated within the period agreed for shipment, enable the buyer to claim the goods from the carrier at the port of destination and, unless otherwise agreed, enable the buyer to sell the goods in transit by the transfer of the document to a subsequent buyer or by notification to the carrier.

When such a transport document is issued in negotiable form and in several originals, a full set of originals must be presented to the buyer.

A9. Checking – packaging – marking

The seller must pay the costs of those checking operations (such as checking quality, measuring, weighing, counting) that are necessary for the purpose of delivering the goods in accordance with A4, as well as the costs of any pre-shipment inspection mandated by the authority of the country of export.

The seller must, at its own expense, package the goods, unless it is usual for the particular trade to transport the type of goods sold unpackaged. The seller may package the goods in the manner appropriate for their transport, unless the buyer has notified the seller of specific packaging requirements before the contract of sale is concluded. Packaging is to be marked appropriately.

A10. Assistance with information and related costs

The seller must, where applicable, in a timely manner, provide to or render assistance in obtaining for the buyer, at the buyer's request, risk and expense, any documents and information, including security-related information, that the buyer needs for the import of the goods and/or for their transport to the final destination.

The seller must reimburse the buyer for all costs and charges incurred by the buyer in providing or rendering assistance in obtaining documents and information as envisaged in B10.

B. THE BUYER'S OBLIGATIONS

B1. General obligations of the buyer

The buyer must pay the price of the goods as provided in the contract of sale.

Any document referred to in B1 – B10 may be an equivalent electronic record or procedure if agreed between the parties or customary.

B2. Licences, authorizations, security clearances and other formalities

Where applicable, it is up to the buyer to obtain, at its own risk and expense, any import licence or other official authorization and carry out all customs formalities for the import of the goods and for their transport through any country.

B3. Contracts of carriage and insurance

a) Contract of carriage

The buyer has no obligation to the seller to make a contract of carriage.

b) Contract of insurance

The buyer has no obligation to the seller to make a contract of insurance. However, the buyer must provide the seller, upon request, with the necessary information for obtaining insurance.

B4. Taking delivery

The buyer must take delivery of the goods when they have been delivered as envisaged in A4 and receive them from the carrier at the named port of destination.

B5. Transfer of risks

The buyer bears all risks of loss of or damage to the goods from the time they have been delivered as envisaged in A4. If the buyer fails to give notice in accordance with B7, then it bears all risks of loss of or damage to the goods from the agreed date or the expiry date of the agreed period for shipment, provided that the goods have been clearly identified as the contract goods.

B6. Allocation of costs

The buyer must, subject to the provisions of A3 a), pay

a) all costs relating to the goods from the time they have been delivered as envisaged in A4, except, where applicable, the costs of customs formalities necessary for export as well as all duties, taxes, and other charges payable upon export as referred to in A6 c);

b) all costs and charges relating to the goods while in transit until their arrival at the port of destination, unless such costs and charges were for the seller's account under the contract of carriage;

c) unloading costs including lighterage and wharfage charges, unless such costs and charges were for the seller's account under the contract of carriage;

d) any additional costs incurred if it fails to give notice in accordance with B7, from the agreed date or the expiry date of the agreed period for shipment, provided that the goods have been clearly identified as the contract goods; and

e) where applicable, all duties, taxes and other charges, as well as the costs of carrying out customs formalities payable upon import of the goods and the costs for their transport through any country unless included within the cost of the contract of carriage.

B7. Notices to the seller

The buyer must, whenever it is entitled to determine the time for shipping the goods and/or the point of receiving the goods within the named port of destination, give the seller sufficient notice thereof.

B8. Proof of delivery

The buyer must accept the transport document provided as envisaged in A8 if it is in conformity with the contract.

B9. Inspection of goods

The buyer must pay the costs of any mandatory pre-shipment inspection, except when such inspection is mandated by the authorities of the country of export.

B10. Assistance with information and related costs

The buyer must, in a timely manner, advise the seller of any security information requirements so that the seller may comply with A10.

The buyer must reimburse the seller for all costs and charges incurred by the seller in providing or rendering assistance in obtaining documents and information as envisaged in A10.

The buyer must, where applicable, in a timely manner, provide to or render assistance in obtaining for the seller, at the seller's request, risk and expense, any documents and information, including security-related information, that the seller needs for the transport and export of the goods and for their transport through any country.

3.2.11 CIF—Cost Insurance and Freight

This rule is to be used only for sea or inland waterway transport.

"Cost Insurance and Freight" means that the seller delivers the goods on board the vessel or procures the goods already so delivered. The risk of loss of or damage to the goods passes when the goods are on board the vessel. The seller must contract for and pay the costs and freight necessary to bring the goods to the named port of destination.

The seller also contracts for insurance cover against the buyer's risk of loss of or damage to the goods during the carriage. The buyer should note that under CIF the seller is required to obtain insurance only on minimum cover. Should the buyer wish to have more insurance protection, it will need either to agree as much expressly with the seller or to make its own extra insurance arrangements.

When CPT, CIP, CFR, or CIF are used, the seller fulfils its obligation to deliver when it hands the goods over to the carrier in the manner specified in the chosen rule and not when the goods reach the place of destination.

This rule has two critical points, because risk passes and costs are transferred at different places. While the contract will always specify a destination port, it might not specify the port of shipment, which is where risk passes to the buyer. If the shipment port is of particular interest to the buyer, the parties are well advised to identify it as precisely as possible in the contract.

The parties are well advised to identify as precisely as possible the point at the agreed port of destination, as the costs to that point are for the account of the seller. The seller is advised to procure contracts of carriage that match this choice precisely. If the seller incurs costs under its contract of carriage related to unloading at the specified point at the port of destination, the seller is not entitled to recover such costs from the buyer unless otherwise agreed between the parties.

The seller is required either to deliver the goods on board the vessel or to procure goods already so delivered for shipment to the destination. In addition the seller is required either to make a contract of carriage or to procure such a contract. The reference to "procure" here caters for multiple sales down a chain ('string sales'), particularly common in the commodity trades.

CIF may not be appropriate where goods are handed over to the carrier before they are on board the vessel, for example goods in containers, which are typically delivered at a terminal. In such circumstances, the CIP rule should be used.

CIF requires the seller to clear the goods for export, where applicable. However, the seller has no obligation to clear the goods for import, pay any import duty or carry out any import customs formalities.

A. THE SELLER'S OBLIGATIONS

A1. General obligations of the seller

The seller must provide the goods and the commercial invoice in conformity with the contract of sale and any other evidence of conformity that may be required by the contract.

Any document referred to in A1 – A10 may be an equivalent electronic record or procedure if agreed between the parties or customary.

A2. Licences, authorizations, security clearances and other formalities

Where applicable, the seller must obtain, at its own risk and expense, any export licence or other official authorization and carry out all customs formalities necessary for the export of the goods.

A3. Contracts of carriage and insurance

a) Contract of carriage

The seller must contract or procure a contract for the carriage of the goods from the agreed point of delivery, if any, at the place of delivery to the named port of destination or, if agreed, any point at that port. The contract of carriage must be made on usual terms at the seller's expense and provide for carriage by the usual route in a vessel of the type normally used for the transport of the type of goods sold.

b) Contract of insurance

The seller must obtain, at its own expense, cargo insurance complying at least with the minimum cover provided by Clauses (C) of the Institute Cargo Clauses (LMA/IUA) or any similar clauses. The insurance shall be contracted with underwriters or an insurance company of good repute and entitle the buyer, or any other person having an insurable interest in the goods, to claim directly from the insurer.

When required by the buyer, the seller shall, subject to the buyer providing any necessary information requested by the seller, provide at the buyer's expense any additional cover, if procurable, such as cover as provided by Clauses (A) or (B) of the Institute Cargo Clauses (LMA/IUA) or any similar clauses and/or cover complying with the Institute War Clauses and/or Institute Strikes Clauses (LMA/IUA) or any similar clauses.

The insurance shall cover, at a minimum, the price provided in the contract plus 10% (i.e., 110%) and shall be in the currency of the contract.

The insurance shall cover the goods from the point of delivery set out in A4 and A5 to at least the named port of destination. The seller must provide the buyer with the insurance policy or other evidence of insurance cover. Moreover, the seller must provide the buyer, at the buyer's request, risk, and expense (if any), with information that the buyer needs to procure any additional insurance.

A4. Delivery

The seller must deliver the goods either by placing them on board the vessel or by procuring the goods so delivered. In either case, the seller must deliver the goods on the agreed date or within the agreed period and in the manner customary at the port.

A5. Transfer of risks

The seller bears all risks of loss of or damage to the goods until they have been delivered in accordance with A4, with the exception of loss or damage in the circumstances described in B5.

A6. Allocation of costs

The seller must pay

a) all costs relating to the goods until they have been delivered in accordance with A4, other than those payable by the buyer as envisaged in B6;

b) the freight and all other costs resulting from A3 a), including the costs of loading the goods on board and any charges for unloading at the agreed port of discharge that were for the seller's account under the contract of carriage;

c) the costs of insurance resulting from A3 b); and

d) where applicable, the costs of customs formalities necessary for export, as well as all duties, taxes and other charges payable upon export, and the costs for their transport through any country that were for the seller's account under the contract of carriage.

A7. Notices to the buyer

The seller must give the buyer any notice needed in order to allow the buyer to take measures that are normally necessary to enable the buyer to take the goods.

A8. Delivery document

The seller must, at its own expense provide the buyer without delay with the usual transport document for the agreed port of destination.

This transport document must cover the contract goods, be dated within the period agreed for shipment, enable the buyer to claim the goods from the carrier at the port of destination and, unless otherwise agreed, enable the buyer to sell the goods in transit by the transfer of the document to a subsequent buyer or by notification to the carrier.

When such a transport document is issued in negotiable form and in several originals, a full set of originals must be presented to the buyer.

A9. Checking – packaging – marking

The seller must pay the costs of those checking operations (such as checking quality, measuring, weighing, counting) that are necessary for the purpose of delivering the goods in accordance with A4, as well as the costs of any pre-shipment inspection mandated by the authority of the country of export.

The seller must, at its own expense, package the goods, unless it is usual for the particular trade to transport the type of goods sold unpackaged. The seller may package the goods in the manner appropriate for their transport, unless the buyer has notified the seller of specific packaging requirements before the contract of sale is concluded. Packaging is to be marked appropriately.

A10. Assistance with information and related costs

The seller must, where applicable, in a timely manner, provide to or render assistance in obtaining for the buyer, at the buyer's request, risk and expense, any documents and information, including security-related information, that the buyer needs for the import of the goods and/or for their transport to the final destination. The seller must reimburse the buyer for all costs and charges incurred by the buyer in providing or rendering assistance in obtaining documents and information as envisaged in B10.

B. THE BUYER'S OBLIGATIONS

B1. General obligations of the buyer

The buyer must pay the price of the goods as provided in the contract of sale.

Any document referred to in B1 – B10 may be an equivalent electronic record or procedure if agreed between the parties or customary.

B2. Licences, authorizations, security clearances and formalities

Where applicable, it is up to the buyer to obtain, at its own risk and expense, any import licence or other official authorization and carry out all customs formalities for the import of the goods and for their transport through any country.

B3. Contracts of carriage and insurance

a) Contract of carriage

The buyer has no obligation to the seller to make a contract of carriage.

b) Contract of insurance

The buyer has no obligation to the seller to make a contract of insurance. However, the buyer must provide the seller, upon request, with any information necessary for the seller to procure any additional insurance requested by the buyer as envisaged in A3 b).

B4. Taking delivery

The buyer must take delivery of the goods when they have been delivered as envisaged in A4 and receive them from the carrier at the named port of destination.

B5. Transfer of risks

The buyer bears all risks of loss of or damage to the goods from the time they have been delivered as envisaged in A4.

If the buyer fails to give notice in accordance with B7, then it bears all risks of loss of or damage to the goods from the agreed date or the expiry date of the agreed period for shipment, provided that the goods have been clearly identified as the contract goods.

B6. Allocation of costs

The buyer must, subject to the provisions of A3 a), pay

a) all costs relating to the goods from the time they have been delivered as envisaged in A4, except, where applicable, the costs of customs formalities necessary for export, as well as all duties, taxes and other charges payable upon export as referred to in A6 d);

b) all costs and charges relating to the goods while in transit until their arrival at the port of destination, unless such costs and charges were for the seller's account under the contract of carriage;

c) unloading costs including lighterage and wharfage charges, unless such costs and charges were for the seller's account under the contract of carriage;

d) any additional costs incurred if it fails to give notice in accordance with B7, from the agreed date or the expiry date of the agreed period for shipment, provided that the goods have been clearly identified as the contract goods;

e) where applicable, all duties, taxes and other charges, as well as the costs of carrying out customs formalities payable upon import of the goods and the costs for their transport through any country, unless included within the cost of the contract of carriage; and

f) the costs of any additional insurance procured at the buyer's request under A3 b) and B3 b).

B7. Notices to the seller

The buyer must, whenever it is entitled to determine the time for shipping the goods and/or the point of receiving the goods within the named port of destination, give the seller sufficient notice thereof.

B8. Proof of delivery

The buyer must accept the transport document provided as envisaged in A8 if it is in conformity with the contract.

B9. Inspection of goods

The buyer must pay the costs of any mandatory pre-shipment inspection, except when such inspection is mandated by the authorities of the country of export.

B10. Assistance with information and related costs

The buyer must, in a timely manner, advise the seller of any security information requirements so that the seller may comply with A10.

The buyer must reimburse the seller for all costs and charges incurred by the seller in providing or rendering assistance in obtaining documents and information as envisaged in A10.

The buyer must, where applicable, in a timely manner, provide to or render assistance in obtaining for the seller, at the seller's request, risk and expense, any documents and information, including security-related information, that the seller needs for the transport and export of the goods and for their transport through any country. (Instruction: all the materials are quoted from https://iccwbo.org/copyright-and-trademarks/)

Exercises

I. Multiple Choice

1. How many international trade terms are included in Incoterms 2010 ________.

A. 10 B. 13

C. 11 D. 9

2. In the following terms, which one means that the seller is not responsible for the export formalities and pay the relevant charge: ________.

A. FCA B. EXW

C. FOB D. FAS

3. According to the amount of the seller's charge, which one is correct: ________.

A. CIF > CFR > FOB B. FOB > CIF > CFR

C. CIF > FOB > CFR D. FOB > CFR > CIF

4. Sellers take the least risk, responsibility and charge ________.

A. DDP B. EXW

C. FCA D. FIB

5. The seller is responsible for import customs declaration ________.

A. EXW B. DDP

C. FOB D. DDU

II. True or False

1. The practice of international trade has been recognized by the world, therefore, it has common legal binding force to the parties in the contract. ( )

2. Under the term of CIF, if the parties haven't pointed out the specific kind of insurance, the sellers could arrange the lowest limit insurance. ( )

3. Under the term of FOB, it doesn't break the contract that, sellers don't have to send shipping advice, if the contract doesn't show the item of "shipping advice". ( )

4. Under the term of CIF, even though the price has includes the freight charge to the destination and premium, the seller doesn't take the responsibility of the goods have to arrive the destination port. ( )

5. Sellers delivering the goods at the pointed place means the sellers transfer the proprietary rights of the goods. ( )

6. One exporter quoted the price of MYM 100 per kilogram, FOB C3%. Now, the customer asked to increase the commission to 5%. If the exporter didn't want to decrease the export net income, should the exporter quoted the price of MYM 101.85 per kilogram, FOB C5%? ( )

7. FOB uses FREIGHT COLLECT as the way to pay freight charge. ( )

8. Under the term of CIF, it is the sellers' obligation to effect insurance; Under the term of CFR, it is the buyers' obligation to effect insurance. While to the two business terms, it is the

buyers' obligation to take the risks in transit. ( )

9. CFR Ex Ship's Hold Rotterdam means the seller should send the goods to Rotterdam, and Delivery at the bottom of the cabin. ( )

10. According to the common practice, it is buyer's obligation to make payment for stowed and trimed if FOB is not followed by stowed and trimmed. ( )

III. Questions

1. What is FOB?
2. What is CIF?
3. What is the buyer's obligation in EXW?
4. What is the seller's obligation in CFB?
5. What are the two new international business terms in Incoterms rules?

Chapter Four　Payment Terms

This part covers the following topics:

4.1　The Brief Introduction of Payment Terms in International Trade;

4.2　The 7 Kinds Commonly Used Payment Terms.

By the end of this part, you will be able to master the following payment terms:

1. T/T (Telegraphic Transfer);
2. L/C (Letter of Credit);
3. D/P (Documents Against Payment);
4. D/A (Documents Against Acceptance);
5. Bill of exchange;
6. Documentary collection;
7. Open account.

4.1　The Brief Introduction of Payment Terms in International Trade

If you have shopped online on international portals or have received payments from abroad, you would have wondered about how the payments flow across the world and which banks and financial institutions underpin global commerce and trade. Further, if you work in a corporate that has global supply chains with international suppliers and customers, you would be again dealing with a complex network of institutions and banks that route the payments from one end of the supply chain or the value chain to the other. In addition, when nations trade with each other and when central banks transact with each other as well as banks in different countries deal with each other, then they are all participating in the international payment system that is the bedrock of global payment flows.

PAYMENT TERMS

So, who and what are the constituents and components of the international payment system? To start with, banks and financial institutions form the first layer of the international payment wherein they hold accounts of other global banks who in turn hold accounts of the former. This enables the banks to send and receive payments from each other as they can simply debit their accounts and credit the other bank's account with them and this in turn leads to payments flowing to the recipient bank that debit the sending bank and credit their account.

Indeed, it can be said that banks such as Citibank which is part of the international financial conglomerate, Citigroup, Standard Chartered, HSBC, and Barclays form the lifeline of the international payment system by routing the money from the senders to the recipients anywhere in the world, anytime of the year, and any place that they are located in.

To succeed in today's global marketplace and win sales against foreign competitors, exporters must offer their customers attractive sales terms supported by the appropriate payment methods. Because getting paid in full and on time is the ultimate goal for each export sale, an appropriate payment method must be chosen carefully to minimize the payment risk while also accommodating the needs of the buyer. There are 7 primary methods of payment for international transactions. During or before contract negotiations, you should consider which method in the figure is mutually desirable for you and your customer.

4.2 The 7 Kinds Commonly Used Payment Terms

4.2.1 T/T (Telegraphic Transfer)

1. The explanation of T/T

The telegraphic transfer is a means of wiring funds from one location to another. Originally, this process made use of the telegraph as a means of transferring money between a point of origin and a point of termination. Today, the process of transferring money between two parties no longer involves the telegraph, but the use of the term remains common in several countries.

Sometimes referred to as a Telex Transfer or simply T/T, the telegraphic transfer has long been a means of communication between banking institutions. In days gone by, the telegraphic transfer could be used to send money from an account in one bank to an account at a bank located anywhere else in the world. Generally, there were charges associated with the performance of a transfer, with both the sender and the recipient paying a small fee for the transaction.

Bangkok Bank

APPLICATION FOR □C/O □D/D □T/T

DATE:________

APPLICANT	
Name:________	
Address:________	
Date of Birth/Place of Birth:________	Telephone No.:________
ID/Business Registration.No.:________	Amount Remitted ________
Occupation & Employer's Name:________	@________ ________
	Commission ________
Nature of Business:________	Postage/Cable ________
	Comm. In Lieu ________
Place of Residence/Place of Incorporntion:________	TOTAL ________
BENEFICIARY	Settlement □Debiting Account No.:________
Name:________	□ Cash:Non-Account Holder(Max. atlowed S$10K)
Address:________	□ Cash:Account Holder(If amount is>S$10K,please provide source of founds):________
	□ Others:For Non-Account Holder and amount>S$20K··
Occupation:________	Purpose of Payment:________
Nature of Business:________	
	Payment Ref:________
Beneficiary's A/C No.:________	Bangkok Bank PCL Singapone Charges
Beneficiary's Bank/Address:________	□ Applicant □ Beneficiary
	Agent Bank TT Charges
Relationship Between Applicent and Beneficiary:________	□ Applicant □ Beneficiary
	□ FX Contract(if Applicable) Value Date:________ Rate:________

AUTHORIZATION AND AGREEMENT:
This application for Cashier's Order/Demand Draft/Telegraphic Transfer(the Application)is made subject to the Terns and Conditions overleaf.I/we have read and agreed to such Terms and Conditions.I/we undertake and agree to furnish to the Bank any and all additional information,particulers and documents as the Bank may require at its absolute discretion before the Bank processes the Application.

For Bank Use	
Aushorised By	Checked By
Bank Ref.No.:	

____
Applicant's Signature
Company Stamp(If Applicable)

CUSTOMER'S COPY

FM-179/08-11

Well into the 20th century, persons could also make use of a telegraphic transfer to move entire balances of funds from one bank to another. For example, a person living in New York City may take a job located in Los Angeles. Rather than withdrawing funds from existing bank accounts and physically transporting the funds across the country, the individual would establish new accounts in Los Angeles and then authorize the two banks involved to transfer all the funds into the new accounts. At that point, the accounts at the New York bank would be closed.

2. Breaking down "Telegraphic Transfer—TT"

Funds sent between institutions are transferred through the Federal Reserve System for U. S. domestic transfers and the Society for Worldwide Interbank Financial Telecommunication (SWIFT) for international transfers. While the term can refer to both U. S. domestic and international transfers, it is most commonly associated with transfers through SWIFT. The use of these systems provides a level of security to the transaction as well as a set of standards and regulations to control how the transfers take place.

Telegraphic Transfers are usually fairly expensive due to the fast nature of the transaction. Generally, the Telegraphic Transfer is complete within two to four business days depending on the origin and destination of the transfer, as well as any currency exchange requirements. The cost associated with a Telegraphic Transfer can also be affected by these variables. Additional factors affecting the cost can include, but are not limited to, the amount being transferred and the institution chosen to complete the transaction. Associated fees to complete the transfer are not standardized across all institutions and therefore can vary dramatically from one institution to the next.

3. Required information

To complete the transfer, certain information regarding the sender and destination are required. Whether a person transfers funds between two accounts that are both held in his name, or between two accounts held by two different individuals, the most pertinent information required for the transfer are the account numbers and information regarding the corresponding financial institutions. Personally identifiablc information is also required for security purposes and to confirm the identity of the sender. Similar requirements are required between business entities, but the identifiable information relates to the business instead of the individual.

4. Transfer mechanism

Originally, as the name suggests, telegraphs were used to communicate the transfer between financial institutions. While the telegraph has become obsolete, as of 2016, the Telegraphic Transfer concept has evolved with changing technologies and uses secure cable networks to transfer funds. At times, the transfer mechanism may be referred to by the more general term, wire transfer, or by the more updated term, electronic funds transfer (ETF).

5. The process of T/T

Telegraphic Transfer, T/T

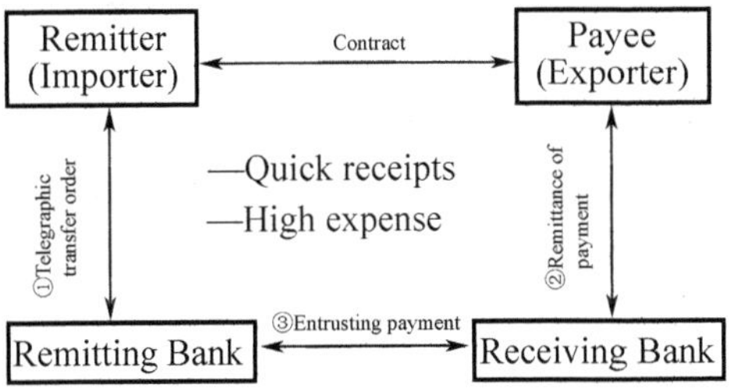

4.2.2 L/C (Letter of Credit)

1. The explanation of L/C

Letters of credit (L/Cs) are one of the most secure instruments available to international traders. An L/C is a commitment by a bank on behalf of the buyer that payment will be made to the exporter, provided that the terms and conditions stated in the L/C have been met, as verified through the presentation of all required documents. The buyer pays his or her bank to render this service. An L/C is useful when reliable credit information about a foreign buyer is difficult to obtain, but the exporter is satisfied with the credit worthiness of the buyer's foreign bank. An L/C also protects the buyer because no payment obligation arises until the goods have been shipped or delivered as promised.

2. Characteristics of credit

- Banker's primary payment liability

  In any event, the credit represents a direct undertaking of bank's primary payment liability to beneficiary, not only the issuing bank, but also the confirming banker. If the documents handed in by beneficiary are in conformity with the credit terms and conditions, the issuing bank should be to make payment to the beneficiary, even if the applicant fails to fulfill his liability. Thus the credit serves almost as a guarantee in that the bank assures payment to the beneficiary so long as he complies with conditions stipulated in the credit.

- Self-sufficient instrument

  A credit, by the nature, is separate transaction from the sales or other contracts on which it may be based and banks are in no way concerned with and bound by such contracts, even if any reference whatsoever to such contracts is included in the credit.

- Banks only deal with documents

  In credit operations all parties concerned deal with documents, and not with goods, services and/or other performances. It is immaterial to them whether the actual merchandise complies with the sales contract. Banks are charged with the responsibility to examine all documents with reasonable care to ascertain that they appear on their face to be in accordance with the terms and conditions of the credit.

APPLICATION FOR IRREVOCABLE LETTER OF CREDIT

COMMERCIAL BANK

Branch: Credit No.:

Date: VAT/BR/NC/TIN NO.:

40A Transferable Credit Yes/No 31D Date of Expiry of the Credit 31D Place of Expiry of the Credit	H.S.CODE: Terms of Delivery (EXW/FOB/CFR/CIF/FCA/CPT/CIP) BOL Registration No.
50 Applicant's Name: Applicant's Addres: Telephome Nos. Fax Nos. E-mail Address. A/C No. Contact person: Mobile No.	46A Documents to be presented by the beneficiary (Please place × where necessary) ☐ Mannully signed commercial invoice in ☐ copies quoting L/C No. H.S. Code Import licence No. ______ and certifying goods are in accordance with Proforma Invoice No. ______ dated ______ Invoices must indicate F.O.B. Value freight and insurance separately. ☐ Bill of lading (Sea) ☐ Air Way Bill (Air) ☐ B/L & AWB ☐ Bill of lading indicate Container Nos ______ ☐ Certificate of ______ origin issued by ______
59 Beneficiary's Name: Beneficiary's Address:	☐ Insurance Policy /Certificate (In duplicate) payable to the order of Commercial Bank of Ceylon Plc. Covering Institute Cargo Clauses A (1.1.82) Institute War Clause Cargo (1.1.82) Institute Strike Clause Cargo (1.1.82) for C.I.F. value plus ______% Claim payable in Colombo Inspective of Percentage ☐ Combined certificate of origin and invoice acceptable

3. Parties to credit

- Applicant

  The applicant for a credit, also referred to as the principal, accounted, or opener, is the party who applies a bank to issue the credit. They are normally importers.

- Issuing bank

  By issuing a credit, the issuing bank undertakes full responsibility for payment.

  The most important liability of the issuing bank is that it must examine all documents to ascertain that they are in accordance with the terms and conditions of the credit. If the documents on their face meet the terms of the credit, the issuing bank has to fulfill its commitment to pay the beneficiary.

- Advising bank

  An advising bank has the task of advising the beneficiary that credit has been issued in his favor, so that the beneficiary may make necessary preparation for the goods and drafting the documents. It only proves the authenticity of the credit and not responsible for other things, such as making payment to the beneficiary.

- Negotiating bank

  A negotiating bank is the bank who ready to pay the documents under the credit. After checking that the documents are in order, the negotiating bank will hold the documents and give the net proceeds to the beneficiary. In this way, the negotiating bank is actually providing financing to the beneficiary. And then, as the holder, the negotiating bank will claim reimbursement from the issuing bank. Throughout this process, the negotiating bank has the right of recourse against the beneficiary, and if the documents are dishonored by the issuing bank or it happened that the issuing bank fell bankrupt, the negotiating bank is entitled to turn to the beneficiary for repayment.

- Paying bank

  A paying bank is the bank who is responsible for payment. It is the issuing bank or it may be another bank appointed by the issuing bank.

- Beneficiary

  The beneficiary is usually the exporter. However, under a credit business, there is no direct relationship that exist between the applicant and the beneficiary. And the bank is only in a relationship with applicant or beneficiary, not with importer and exporter.

4. The process of L/C

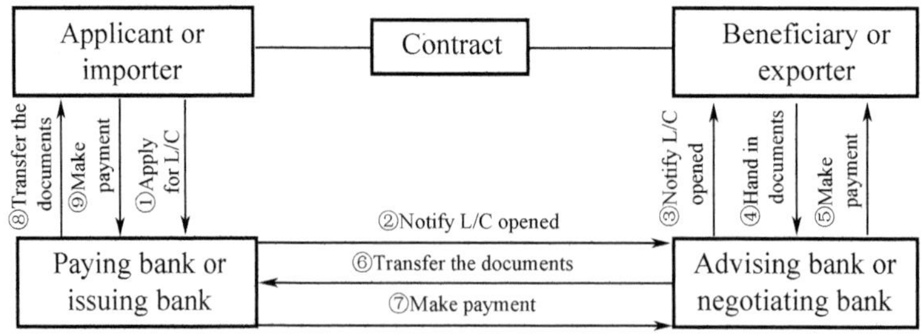

5. Advantages and disadvantages of L/C

- Advantages

It satisfies the financing needs of the seller and the buyer by placing the bank's credit standing.

It may allow the buyer to obtain a lower purchase price for the goods as well as longer payment terms.

It reduces the commercial credit risk since payment is assured by the bank which issues an irrevocable documentary credit. The seller no longer needs to rely on the willingness and capability of the buyer to make payment.

It expands sources of supply for the buyers since certain sellers are willing to sell only against cash in advance or a documentary credit.

- Disadvantages

It is costly and cumbersome to set up.

It does not guarantee against all possible risks, importers sometimes can gain goods before paying for them.

Technical errors in the documents can cause non-payment.

Some importers complaint the quality of goods.

6. Kinds of L/C

- Irrevocable L/C

The irrevocable L/C means that once the L/C is opened, without agreement of the beneficiary, the opening bank cannot amend or revoke the L/C within its validity. As long as the beneficiary provides the documents in accordance with the stipulation in the L/C, the opening bank shall perform its duty of payment.

- Revocable L/C

The revocable L/C means that the opening bank may amend or revoke the credit before negotiation, acceptance or payment without agreement of the beneficiary.

- Documentary

The documentary L/C stipulates that the bill of exchange drawn by the seller should be accompanied with shipping documents. This kind of L/C is the most widely used in international trade.

- Clean L/C

If the bill of exchange is a clean bill, the L/C is called a clean L/C.

- Confirmed L/C

The confirmed L/C should be an irrevocable L/C confirmed by another bank named by the opening bank. Once an L/C is confirmed, there are two banks to be responsible for payment of the purchase price, they are opening bank and confirming bank.

4.2.3 D/P (Documents Against Payment)

1. The explanation of D/P

A terms of payment arrangement in which an exporter entrusts the ownership documents of an asset to his/her bank, which then presents them to an importer only after the bank has received payment for the asset. Essentially, the bank holds hostage the ownership documents, which the importer needs to take possession of the merchandise, until the bank, and, by extension, the exporter, are paid. A risk for the exporter is the possibility that the importer will refuse to pay, and, while he/she will not be able to take possession of the merchandise, the exporter has little legal recourse. The terms of this agreement are set between the importer and exporter at the time of the sale.

The D/P transaction utilizes a sight draft. Payment is on demand.

After the goods are shipped, the exporter sends the sight draft to the clearing bank, along with documents necessary for the importer/buyer to obtain the goods from customs. The buyer has to settle the payment with the bank before the documents are released and he can take delivery of the goods. If the buyer fails or refuses to pay, the exporter has the right to recover the goods and resell them.

On the surface, D/P transactions seem fairly safe from the seller's perspective. However, in practice there are risks involved.

- The buyer can refuse to honor payment on any grounds.
- When the goods are shipped long distances, say from Hong Kong to the United States, it is usually impractical and too expensive for the seller to ship them back home. Thus, the seller is forced to sell the goods in the original country of destination at what is usually a heavy discount.
- In cases of shipments by air freight, it is possible that the buyer will actually receive the goods before going to the bank and paying for them.

2. The process of D/P

Documents Against Payment, D/P

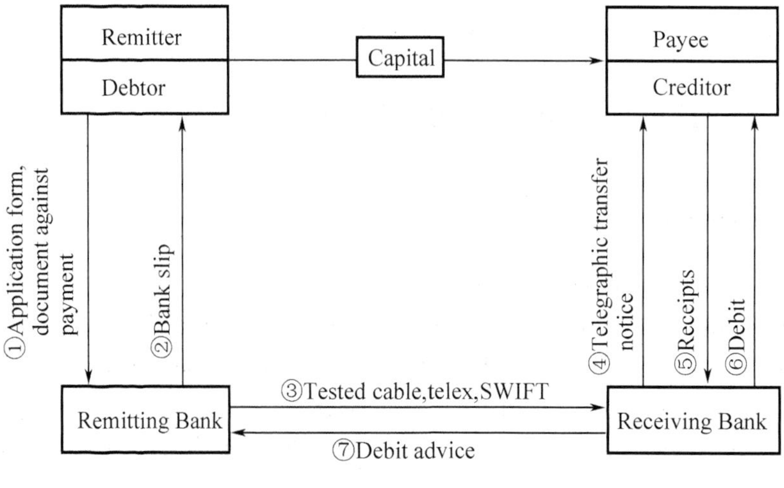

4.2.4 D/A (Documents Against Acceptance)

1. The explanation of D/A

D/A means documents against acceptance. It is a form of payment agreement between an exporter and importer. Upon delivery or shipment of items the exporter prepares shipping documents like bill of lading, commercial invoice, packing list, bill of exchange or bank draft. These documents are sent to the bank of the importer. Upon arrival of goods to the country of the importer, the importer will get the shipping documents. When the importer accepts the shipment and signs the bill of exchange or bank draft, then the exporter can collect the payment and the importer pays the bank.

The D/A transaction utilizes a term or time draft. In this case, the documents required to take possession of the goods are released by the clearing bank only after the buyer accepts a time draft drawn upon him. In essence, this is a deferred payment or credit arrangement. The buyer's assent is referred to as a trade acceptance.

D/A terms are usually after sight, for instance "at 90 days sight", or after a specific date, such as "at 150 days bill of lading date."

As with open account terms, there are some inherent risks in selling on D/A:

- As with a D/P, the importer can refuse to accept the goods for any reason, even if they are in good condition.
- The buyer can default on the payment of a trade acceptance. Unless it has been guaranteed by the clearing bank, the seller will need to institute collection procedures and/or legal action.

2. The process of D/A

Documents Against Acceptance,D/A

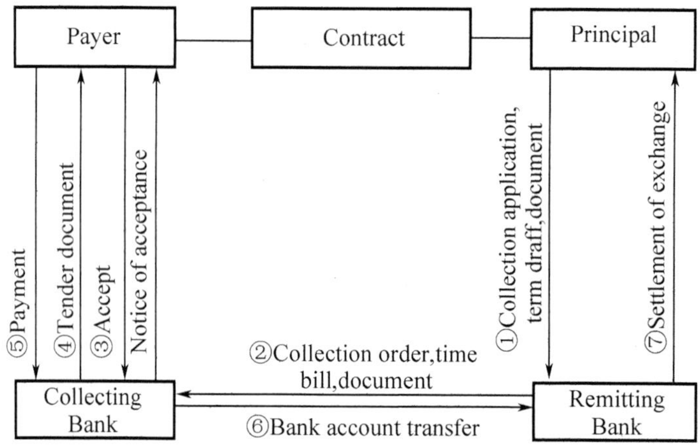

4.2.5 Bill of Exchange

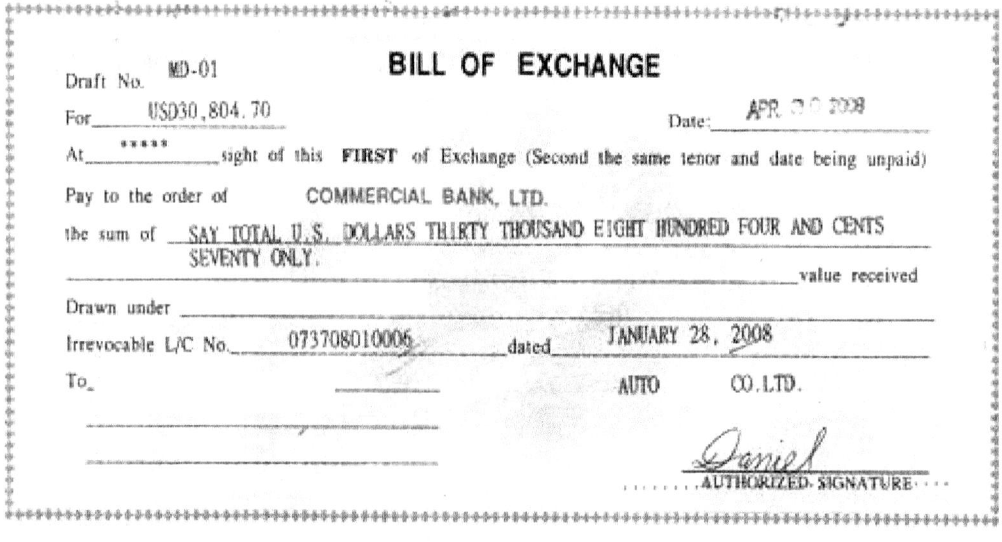

BILL OF EXCHANGE

Draft No. MD-01

For USD30,804.70 Date: APR. [illegible] 2008

At ***** sight of this FIRST of Exchange (Second the same tenor and date being unpaid)

Pay to the order of COMMERCIAL BANK, LTD.

the sum of SAY TOTAL U.S. DOLLARS THIRTY THOUSAND EIGHT HUNDRED FOUR AND CENTS SEVENTY ONLY. value received

Drawn under

Irrevocable L/C No. 073708010006 dated JANUARY 28, 2008

To AUTO CO.LTD.

Daniel

AUTHORIZED SIGNATURE

1. The explanation of bill of exchange

A bill of exchange is a written order used primarily in international trade that binds one party to pay a fixed sum of money to another party on demand or at a predetermined date. It is a negotiable instrument that is both drawn up by and made payable to the exporter/seller. Although written by the seller, it has the equivalent effect of a check written by the buyer.

Bills of exchange are similar to checks and promissory notes. They can be drawn by individuals or banks and are generally transferable by endorsements. The difference between a promissory note and a bill of exchange is that the latter is transferable and can bind one party to pay a third party that was not involved in its creation.

There are up to three parties involved in a bill of exchange transaction. The drawee is the party that pays the sum specified by the bill of exchange. The payee is the one who receives that sum. The drawer is the party that obliges the drawee to pay the payee. The drawer and the payee are the same entity, unless the drawer transfers the bill of exchange to a third-party payee.

Drawer—the party issuing the bill of exchange; usually the exporter/seller.

Drawee—the recipient of the bill of exchange for payment or acceptance; usually the buyer.

Payee—the party to whom the bill is payable; usually the seller's bank. Bills of exchange are either payable at sight (sight drafts) where the bank pays the full amount upon presentation, or payable at some future date (time or term drafts).

Bills of exchange generally do not pay interest, making them in essence post-dated checks. They may accrue interest if not paid by a certain date, however, in which case the rate must be specified on the instrument. They can, conversely, be transferred at a discount before the date specified for payment.

If these bills are issued by a bank, they can be referred to as bank drafts. If they are issued by individuals, they can be referred to as trade drafts. If the funds are to be paid immediately or on demand, the bill of exchange is known as a sight bill; if they are to be paid at a set date in the future, it is known as a term bill.

2. The process of bill of exchange

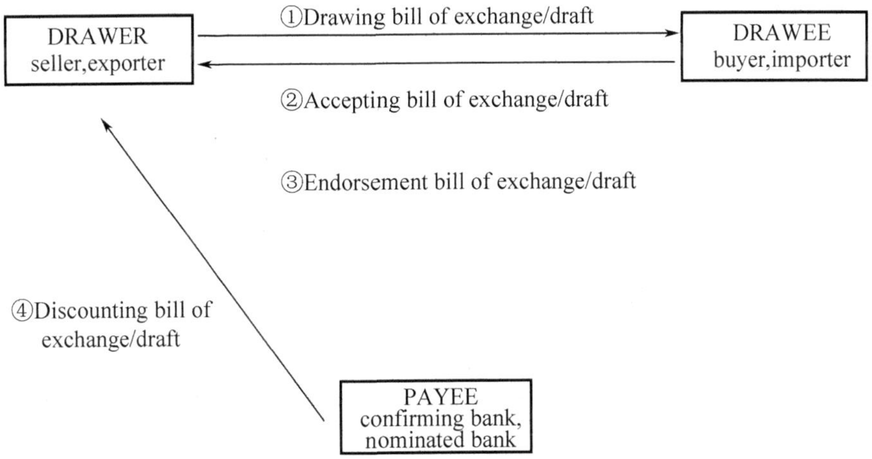

4.2.6 Documentary Collection

1. The explanation of documentary collection

A documentary collection is a trade transaction in which the exporter hands over the task of collecting payment for goods supplied to his or her bank, which sends the shipping documents to the importer's bank together with payment instructions. A documentary collection (D/C) is so-called because the exporter receives payment from the importer in exchange for the shipping documents, with the funds and documents channeled through their respective banks. While D/Cs are less complicated and cheaper than letters of credit, they are riskier for exporters because they do not have a verification process and offer limited recourse if the importer does not pay. They are therefore only recommended in situations where the exporter and importer have a long-standing trade relationship.

A key document in documentary collections is the bill of exchange or draft, which is a formal demand for payment from the exporter to importer. D/Cs can be classified into two types, depending on when payment is sought by the exporter: 1) documents against payment (D/P), which requires the importer to pay the face amount of the draft at sight, or 2) documents against acceptance (D/A), which requires the importer to pay on a specified future date.

In a D/P collection, the exporter ships the goods and then gives the shipping documents to his or her bank (which is also known as the remitting bank). The bank forwards these documents to the importer's bank (known as the collecting bank), which will only release the documents to the importer on receipt of payment for the goods. The collecting bank then remits the funds to the exporter's bank for payment to the exporter.

A D/A collection differs from a D/P collection because the exporter extends credit to the importer through a time draft in the former case. Once the importer signs the time draft—which becomes a binding obligation to pay by the due date shown on the draft because of the signed acceptance—the documents are released to the importer. The collecting bank contacts the importer on the due date for payment, which upon receipt is remitted to the exporter's bank for payment to the exporter.

The exporter's risk is obviously higher in the D/A collection process, since the exporter has no control over the goods after the importer's acceptance and may not get paid for them.

In terms of risk, D/Cs are much safer than an open account but have fewer safeguards than a letter of credit, since the banks neither guarantee payment nor verify document accuracy and authenticity. These features can be exploited by fraudsters posing as either the exporter or importer. As a result, D/Cs are not recommended for exports to nations that are politically or economically unstable. Overall, because of their lower cost and simple process, D/Cs are best suited for established trade relationships in sound export markets, and for transactions involving ocean shipments rather than air or land shipments which are more difficult to control.

2. The process of documentary collection

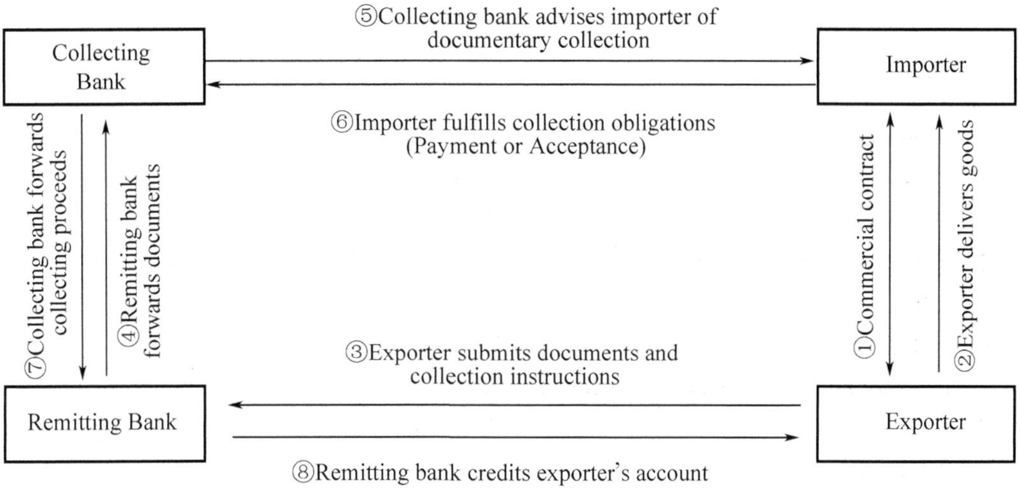

4.2.7 Open Account

1. The explanation of open account

An open account transaction is a sale where the goods are shipped and delivered before payment is due, which is usually in 30 to 90 days. Obviously, this option is the most advantageous option to the importer in terms of cash flow and cost, but it is consequently the highest risk option for an exporter. Because of intense competition in export markets, foreign buyers often press exporters for open account terms since the extension of credit by the seller to the buyer is more common abroad. Therefore, exporters who are reluctant to extend credit may lose a sale to their competitors. However, the exporter can offer competitive open account terms while substantially mitigating the risk of non-payment by using of one or more of the appropriate trade finance techniques, such as export credit insurance.

2. The process of open account

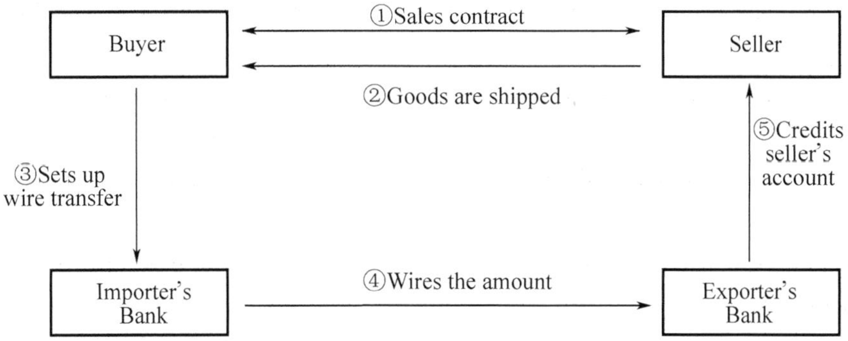

Exercises

I. Multiple Choice

1. Which does the payment term need bank's guarantee? ________.

A. L/C　　B. D/A

C. D/P　　D. T/T

2. In the following payment terms, which one does the seller take more risks? ________.

A. L/C　　B. D/A

C. D/P　　D. T/T

3. What is the another name for buyer in L/C? ________.

A. Beneficiary　　B. Dealer

C. Applicant　　D. Buyer

4. Under which condition, does the bank refuse to make payment? ________.

A. The buyer and the seller have other business financial matters waiting to be paid

B. There are differences between the bill of loading and the contract

C. The quality of the goods are not the same with the contract

D. The quantity of the goods are not the same with the contract

5. L/C means ________.

A. Letter of Credit　　B. Letter of Cash

C. Load of Credit　　D. Load of Cash

II. True or False

1. The bank has the right of refusing to pay if the documents are presented later than the validity of L/C. (　　)

2. Exporters always insist on payment by cash in advance when they are trading with old customers. (　　)

3. The issuing bank bears the prime liability for payment in the letter of credit. (　　)

4. Banks deal in documents instead of goods, therefore, they are only concerned that documents presented appear on their face to comply with the terms and conditions of the documentary credits.

5. Documentary credits are the most ideal method of payment to provide security for both buyers and sellers. (　　)

6. A letter of credit is a conditional undertaking to make payment in the case of conformity. (　　)

7. An issuance of the letter of credit, the issuing bank may refuse payment if the applicant becomes bankrupt. (　　)

8. The issuing bank should be located in the importer's country, while the advising bank should be located in exporter's country. (　　)

9. It is necessary for the buyer to clearly specify a period of validity of the L/C when applying for the opening of L/C. ( )

10. Confirmation to credit may be given by an advising bank at the request of the issuing bank. ( )

III. Questions

1. Could you describe the procedure of T/T?
2. What is the difference between D/P and D/A?
3. Could you describe the procedure of L/C?
4. What are the contents of L/C?
5. Could you briefly state the procedure of D/P?

Chapter Five International Cargo Transportation

This part covers the following topics:

5.1 Types of Transport;
5.2 Documents in Cargo Transportation;
5.3 Clause of Shipment.

By the end of this part, you will be able to master:

1. Different types of transportation;
2. Ocean transport and container transport;
3. Different documents needed in different modes of transportation;
4. Different documents' characteristics;
5. The content of clauses relating to cargo transportation;
6. Classification of bill of lading.

In International trade, several modes of transportation can be used to move goods from one country to another country. These modes vary in cost, in speed and in other aspects. Usually, a trader has the choice of many different forms of transport by land, sea, or air. Each form has its own particular advantages and disadvantages and the trader must wisely make their choice. Often, a combination of these forms may be used so as to complete the distribution in a timely and cost-efficient manner. Each form has its own basis of charging freight and its own documentation.

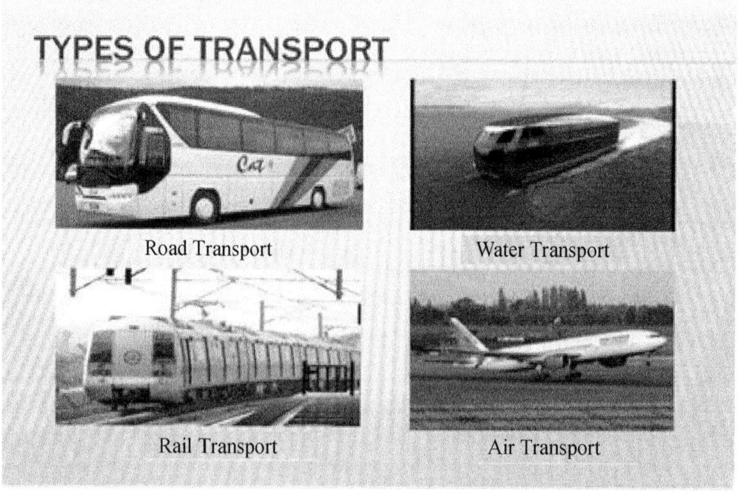

5.1 Types of Transport

Types of transport is a term used to distinguish substantially different ways to perform. The different modes of transport are air, water, and land transport, which includes rail, road and off-road transport. Other modes also exist, including pipelines, cable transport, and space transport. Human-powered transport and animal-powered transport are sometimes regarded as their own mode, but these normally also fall into the other categories. In general, transportation is used for the movement of people, animals, and other things. Each mode of transport has a fundamentally different technological solution, and some require a separate environment. Each mode has its own infrastructure, vehicles, and operations.

5.1.1 Water Transport

Water transport is the process of transport that a watercraft, such as a barge, boat, ship or sailboat, makes over a body of water, such as a sea, ocean, lake, canal or river. If a boat or other vessel can successfully pass through a waterway it is known as a navigable waterway. The need for buoyancy unites watercraft, and makes the hull a dominant aspect of its construction, maintenance and appearance. When a boat is floating on the water the hull of the boat is pushing aside water where the hull now is, this is known as displacement. Although slow, modern sea transport is a highly effective method of transporting large quantities of non-perishable goods. Commercial vessels, nearly 35,000 in number, carried 7.4 billion tons of cargo in 2007. Transport by water is significantly less costly than air transport for transcontinental shipping; short sea shipping and ferries remain viable in coastal areas.

1. Sea transportation

Sea transportation includes ocean shipping and coastal shipping. Ocean shipping transports goods across the seas of the world, while coastal shipping transports goods between the chief ports of country. There are many different kinds of ships, which can be divided into two main groups: tramp vessels and liners.

(1) Tramp vessels

A tramp has no fixed run but will go wherever a suitable cargo takes it. Thus a ship and crew may be chartered from the ship owner to fetch a cargo of grain from Canada to Latvia, the ship may then be required to carry a cargo of coal from Britain to Melanesia. Bulk carriers and some cruise ships are examples of ships built to operate in this manner.

(2) Liners

A ship may also be categorized as to how it is operated. A liner will have a regular run and operate to a schedule. The scheduled operation requires that such ships are better equipped to deal with causes of potential delay such as bad weather. They are generally higher powered than tramp ships with better seakeeping qualities, thus they are significantly more expensive to build. Liners are typically built for passenger and container operation though past common uses also included mail and general cargo.

2. Inland water transport

Inland water transport is a viable alternative or addition to road and rail transport on European corridors. Though environmentally—friendly and, frequently, the most economical mode of inland transport, it remains largely under—exploited in Europe. Compared with land transport, water transport is low in cost, and is particularly suitable for the movement of heavy, relatively cheap goods. But there are disadvantages for inland water transport in that the speed is sometimes restricted because of the narrow waterways, and the goods can only be directly delivered to places situated on the sides of rivers or canals.

5.1.2 Land Transportation

Land transport covers all land-based transportation systems that provide for the movement of people, goods and services. Land transport plays a vital role in linking communities to each other. Land transport is a key factor in urban planning. It consists of 2 kinds, rail and road.

1. Road transport

A road is an identifiable route of travel, usually surfaced with gravel, asphalt or concrete, and supporting land passage by foot or by a number of vehicles. The most common road vehicle in the developed world is the automobile, a wheeled passenger vehicle that carries its own motor. Transportation by road is flexible, cheap and speedy. Motorcars offer high flexibility, but are deemed with high energy and area use, and the main source of noise and air pollution in cities; buses allow for more efficient travel at the cost of reduced flexibility. Road transport by truck is often the initial and final stage of freight transport. Roads are faster than railways and aircraft for short journey. By the time goods are taken to the station or airport, loaded, unloaded and taken to their destination, the journey could have been made in less time by transporting directly in a road vehicle.

2. Rail transport

Rail transport is a means of conveyance of passengers and goods by way of wheeled vehicles running on rail track, known as a railway or railroad. The rails are anchored perpendicular to railroad train consists of one or more connected vehicles that run on the rails. Propulsion is commonly provided by a locomotive, that hauls a series of unpowered cars, that can carry passengers or freight. The locomotive can be powered by steam, diesel or by electricity supplied by trackside systems. Alternatively, some or all the cars can be powered, known as a multiple unit. Also, a train can be powered by horses, cables, gravity, pneumatics and gas turbines. Railed vehicles move with much less friction than rubber tires on paved roads, making trains more energy efficient, though not as efficient as ships. Railways have advantages over motor vehicles in that they are good for the transport of large quantities of heavy, bulky goods and faster than road transport over long journeys. Rail freight charges become cheaper with distance and weight. The charger per mile falls as the distance increases, and heavy bulk goods such as coal can be carried relatively cheaply.

Nowadays, competition has been a major factor in pushing rates generally downward. Intercity trains are long-haul services connecting cities; modern high-speed rail is capable of speeds up to 430 km/h, but this requires a specially built track. Regional and commuter trains feed cities from suburbs and surrounding areas, while intra-urban transport is performed by high-capacity tramways and rapid transits, often making up the backbone of a city's public transport. Freight trains traditionally used box cars, requiring manual loading and unloading of the cargo. Since the 1960s, container trains have become the dominant solution for general freight, while large quantities of bulk are transported by dedicated trains.

5.1.3 Air Transport

A fixed-wing aircraft, typically airplane, is a heavier-than-air flight vehicle, in which the special geometry of the wing generates lift. Fixed-wing aircraft ranges from small trainers and recreational aircraft to large airliners and military cargo aircraft. For short distances or in places without runways, helicopters can be practical. Air transport is the second fastest method of transport, after space travel. Commercial jets reach speeds of up to 955 kilometres per hour (593 mph) and a considerably higher ground speed if there is a jet stream tailwind, while piston-powered general aviation aircraft may reach up to 555 kilometres per hour (345 mph) or more.

Air transport is suitable for the carriage of high-value, low-bulk goods. If a business can rely on an express courier service for bringing in raw materials, the expense of the air freight can be offset by savings on the cos of holding stock. Freight rates are based on weight and are not affected by the value of the goods. The principle advantage of air transport is speed, which means shorter periods of insurance cover are required than for sea transport, therefore insurance charges are relatively cheaper. And aircraft can travel long distances over land and sea without unloading and reloading. The danger of damage to delicate articles is reduced; insurance rates may be lower than those charged for sea transport in that shorter period of insurance cover is required than for sea transport and goods sent by air do not require packing in heavy and costly crates and lighter packing may save customs duties when these are levied on weight. But bad weather may restrict flights, costly airports are required and goods may have to take a considerable distance by road or rail before and after the flight.

5.1.4 Shipping Container

A shipping container is a container with strength suitable to withstand shipment, storage, and handling. Shipping containers range from large reusable steel boxes used for intermodal shipments to the ubiquitous corrugated boxes. In the context of international shipping trade, "container" or "shipping container" is virtually synonymous with "(standard) intermodal freight container" (a container designed to be moved from one mode of transport to another without unloading and reloading).

(1) Intermodal freight containers

Freight containers are a reusable transport and storage unit for moving products and raw materials between locations or countries. There are about seventeen million intermodal containers in the world, and a large proportion of the world's long-distance freight generated by international trade is transported in shipping containers. In addition, it is estimated that several million of these containers have now been discarded due to the shipping cost of sending them back to their port of origin. Their invention made a major contribution to the globalization of commerce in the second half of the 20th century, dramatically reducing the cost of transporting goods and hence of long-distance trade.

(2) Corrugated box

Corrugated boxes are commonly used as shipping containers (more than 90% of all shipping containers are of this type). They are made of corrugated fiberboard which is lightweight, recyclable, and strong enough to ship a variety of products.

(3) Wooden box

Wooden boxes are often used for shipping heavy and dense products. They are sometimes specified for shipments of government or military shipments.

(4) Crate

A crate is a large container, often made of wood, used to transport large, heavy or awkward items. A crate has a self-supporting structure, with or without sheathing

(5) Intermediate bulk shipping container

An Intermediate bulk container (IBC) is a container used for transport and storage of fluids and bulk materials. The construction may be plastic, composite, steel, stainless steel, etc. Some are foldable (collapsible).

(6) Flexible Intermediate Bulk Container

A Flexible Intermediate Bulk Container, FIBC, big bag, bulk bag, or super sack is a standardized container in large dimensions for storing and transporting and storing granular products. It is often made of a woven synthetic material.

(7) Bulk box

A bulk box, bulk bin, skid box, or tote box is a pallet size box used for storage and shipping of bulk quantities.

(8) Drum

Drums are cylindrical shipping containers made of steel, plastic or fiber. They are often used for liquids and granular materials.

(9) Insulated shipping containers

Insulated shipping containers are a type of packaging used to ship temperature sensitive products such as foods, pharmaceuticals, and chemicals. They are used as part of a cold chain to help maintain product freshness and efficacy.

(10) Pail

Some pails are used as shipping containers.

(11) Unit load device

A Unit Load Device, or ULD, is a container used to transport cargo on commercial aircraft. A ULD can be a pallet or container used to load luggage, freight, and mail on wide-body aircraft and specific narrow-body aircraft. It allows a large quantity of cargo to be bundled into a single unit. Since this leads to fewer units to load, it saves ground crews time and effort and helps prevent delayed flights. Each ULD has its own packing list, manifest, or tracking identification to improve control and tracking of contents

(12) Specialized shipping containers

Custom containers are used for shipments of products such as weapons and aviation components. Customized cushioning, blocking and bracing, carrying handles, lift rings, locks, etc. are common to facilitate handling and to protect the contents. Often, these shipping containers are reusable.

Specialized shipping containers include: high cube containers (providing an extra 1 ft (305 mm) in height to standard shipping containers), pallet wides, open tops, side loaders, double door or tunnel-tainers, and temperature controlled containers.

Another specialized container, known as Transtainer, is a portable fuel and oil freight container. The hybrid bulk fuel tank is originally intended for the construction, mining, logging and farming sectors. The tank can be used to transport and store bulk fuels as well as dangerous liquids, by road, rail and sea.

5.2 Documents in Cargo Transportation

A transport document is a kind of document used to convey information about cargo that is being transported. Kinds of transport documents include: Air Waybill, a transport document used for air freight; Bill of Lading, a transport document for sea freight; CMR (transport document), a transport document for road freight for use in all European countries, as well as additional countries in Asia and Africa.

5.2.1 Shipping Note

A document used in shipping goods by sea. In the case of free goods the shipping notes are the receiving note, addressed by the shipper to the chief officer of the vessel, requesting him to receive on board specified goods, and a receipt for the mate to sign, on receiving whose signature it is called the mate's receipt, and is surrendered by the shipper for the bills of lading.

5.2.2 Bill of Lading

Bill of Lading

<table>
<tr><td>Ship From</td><td colspan="2">Date</td></tr>
<tr><td>Address lines here
Second line here
City, State.
Contact No:
Fax Number:</td><td colspan="2">Sender Name
Unit No:
NOC No:</td></tr>
<tr><td>Ship To</td><td colspan="2" rowspan="2">Approval Note:</td></tr>
<tr><td>Address lines here
Second line here
City, State.
Contact No:
Fax Number:</td></tr>
<tr><td colspan="3">Shipping Organization Information</td></tr>
<tr><td>Description</td><td>QTY</td><td>Unit</td></tr>
<tr><td></td><td></td><td></td></tr>
<tr><td></td><td></td><td></td></tr>
<tr><td></td><td></td><td></td></tr>
<tr><td></td><td></td><td></td></tr>
<tr><td></td><td></td><td></td></tr>
<tr><td>Shipper</td><td colspan="2">Signature of authorized</td></tr>
<tr><td>Signature</td><td colspan="2"></td></tr>
</table>

Bill of Lading Template

A bill of lading (sometimes abbreviated as B/L or BoL) is a document issued by a carrier (or his agent) to acknowledge receipt of cargo for shipment. In British English the term relates to ship transport only, and in American English to any type of transportation of goods. A bill of lading must be negotiable, and serves three main functions: it is a conclusive receipt, i.e. an acknowledgement that the goods have been loaded; and it contains or evidences the terms of the contract of carriage; and it serves as a document of title to the goods, subject to the nemo date rule.

You must prepare and submit a Shipper's Letter of Instructions form to your freight forwarder so that they can issue an accurate bill of lading. This form indicates if the transaction is being made against a letter of credit, whether insurance is required and where to send documents, etc. Once you've finalized terms of payment with your customer, you will be able to furnish these facts to your freight forwarder. Most bills of lading are issued with three originals and several copies.

Bills of lading are one of three crucial documents used in international trade to ensure that exporters receive payment and importers receive the merchandise. The other two documents are a policy of insurance and an invoice. Whereas a bill of lading is negotiable, both a policy and an invoice are assignable.

Depending on how fast you want to get cargo to your customer and how much he or she is willing to spend, you might ship by ocean or air. Accordingly, there are two types of bills of lading, the ocean bill of lading and the airway bill.

1. Ocean bill of lading

An ocean bill of lading serves both as a receipt for the cargo and as a contract for transportation between you (the exporter) and the carrier. It also symbolizes ownership; accordingly, if in negotiable form, it can be bought, sold or traded while the goods are in transit.

We will be covering ocean bills of lading in detail because ocean freight is the most economical—and therefore the most frequently used—method of export shipment. There are numerous different types of ocean bill of lading, but you will find that the following are the most commonly used:

(1) Shipped (on board) bill of lading

An "on-board bill of lading" is issued when the cargo has been placed aboard the named vessel. It is signed and certified by the master of the vessel. For a letter of credit transaction, this bill of lading is required for you (the exporter) to get paid. An on-board bill of lading denotes that merchandise has been physically loaded onto a shipping vessel, such as a freighter or cargo plane. It confirms the goods are actually on board the vessel.

(2) Received for shipment bill of lading

A received for shipment bill of lading denotes that merchandise has been received, but is not guaranteed to have already been loaded onto a shipping vessel. (Typically, it will be issued by a freight-forwarder at a port or depot). Such bills can be converted upon being loaded.

(3) Clean bill of lading & Unclean bill of lading

Clean bill of lading: If the statement "in apparent good order and condition" is not modified by the shop-owner, then the bill of lading is regarded as "clean". By issuing clean bill of lading, the ship-owner admits his full liability of the cargo described in the bill. A "clean bill of lading" is issued when the shipment is received in good order. If there is any damage or a shortage of product is found, a clean bill of lading will not be issued.

Unclean bill of lading: If the ship-owner does not agree with any of the statements made in the bill of lading, he will add a clause to this effect, thereby causing the bill of lading to be termed as "unclean", "foul", "dirty". The clauses of this kind are many including: inadequate packaging, second-hand cases, damaged crates etc. this kind of bill of lading is usually unacceptable by a bank.

(4) Negotiable bill of lading& Non-Negotiable bill of lading

Negotiable bill of lading: Basically the bill of lading is a negotiable document which allows the goods to be transferred by endorsement. A "shipper's order" (negotiable) bill of lading is used when you want to impose conditions on delivery of the goods, such as acceptance of a draft. This type of bill of lading works well when payment has been secured by a letter of credit because you can make sure that the terms of the L/C are met before the goods are released.

Non-Negotiable bill of lading: In this case, the consignee (or other named party) cannot transfer the property or goods by transfer the bills. This particular type is seldom found and will normally apply when goods are shipped on a non-commercial basis. A "straight" (non-negotiable) bill of lading provides for delivery to the person whose name appears on it. It must be marked "non-negotiable." Only the person named can claim the goods upon arrival. This type of bill is usually used for goods shipped on an open-account payment basis when the exporter is not concerned about the importer receiving the goods without payment.

(5) Container bill of lading

Container bill of lading is a document that gives information about the goods being transported in a container or containers from one port to another. They cover the goods from port-to-port or from inland point of departure to inland point of destination.

(6) Through bills of lading

In many cases it is necessary to employ two or more carriers to get the goods to their final destination. The carriage therefore may be either by a second vessel or by a different form of transport.

(7) Transshipment bill of lading

This type is used usually by shipping companies when there is no direct service between two ports.

(8) Stale bill of lading

Bills presented to the consignee or buyer or his bank after the goods are due at the port are said to be stale. A cargo cannot normally be collected by the buyer without the bill of lading and the late arrival of this document may have undesirable consequences such as warehouse rent, etc.

(9) Packing List and Weight List

Packing list is an international trade document, used to identify details of the shipment in terms of packaging. Packing list normally should not disclose any financial information regarding the shipment such as total amount of the cargo, unit price of the items or payments terms. Weight list merely gives details of the weight of the consignment. In some countries, a weight list document is required for import.

2. Airway bill

When you use air freight, an airway bill is issued in lieu of a bill of lading. It serves as a through bill of lading which covers domestic and international flights moving cargo to a specific destination. Your air transportation carrier will advise you of the house airway bill number and the master airway bill number assigned to your shipment. You must be sure to communicate these to your customer along with other transportation details.

Airway bills serve functions similar to those of ocean bills of lading, but they are only issued in non-negotiable form. It means that you and your bank have less protection because you lose title to the goods once shipment commences. Be sure to check with your logistics expert if you are shipping hazardous goods. Special forms are required. The air waybill is the most important document issued by a carrier either directly or through its authorized agent. It is a non-negotiable transport document that covers transport of cargo from airport to airport. By accepting a shipment, an IATA cargo agent is acting on behalf of the carrier whose air waybill is issued. Air waybills have eleven digit numbers which can be used to make bookings, check the status of delivery, and current position of the shipment.

Air waybills are issued in eight sets of different colors. The first three copies are classified as originals. The first original, green in color, is the issuing carrier's copy. The second, colored pink, is the consignee's copy. The third, colored blue, is the shipper's copy. A fourth brown copy acts as the Delivery Receipt, or proof of delivery. The other three copies are white.

3. Consignment note

A shipping agreement between the consignor of a shipment and the carrier of the shipment, which records the receipt of goods for shipment to a specified destination. The consignment note also specifies the consignee of the shipment and the fee for shipment, but unlike a bill of lading, is not a document of title. Also called a waybill.

4. Parcel post receipt

Parcel post receipt is issued by the post office for goods set by parcel post. It is both a receipt and evidence of dispatch. It is not a document of title and goods should be consigned to the party specified in the documentary credit. An airmail label should be fixed to a postal receipt in respect of air parcel post dispatch, ad the post office should stamp the receipt "air parcel". It is a cheap method of delivery for small consignments and the post office can provide insurance if required.

5.3 Clauses of Shipment

Transport clause is a part of a contract. They include the time of shipment, the port of departure, the port of destination and shipment notice etc.

5.3.1 Time of Shipment

One of the main clauses in a contract is the clause in respect of the shipment. The shipment date should be made in such a manner that it facilitates the seller and enables the seller to effect shipment on time and perform the relevant obligations stipulated in the contract.

Different shipment period should be fixed, based on the availability of shipping space, for contracted goods of different nature. An unreasonable short time for shipment shall cause no little inconvenience to the seller.

There are several ways to decide the time of shipment according to the date of letter of credit.

(1) The deadline method. We can see clause like "shipment before 5th October, 2015 from Shanghai to Manchester port, USA".

(2) The duration period. "shipment during March/April/May", "shipment during October/November 2016 in two equally monthly lots".

(3) The letter of credit method. "shipment with 30 days after receipt of L/C which must reach the seller no later than the end of October, 216 failing which the seller reserves the right to cancel this contract without further notice, or to lodge claims for direct losses sustained from." Under this method, because of the use of letter of credit, the seller should stipulate when the letter of credit should reach the seller by using sentences like "the buyer must open the relative L/C to reach the seller before October 15th 2016". Otherwise, the seller cannot arrange production, packing and shipping and thus e in a passive position.

5.3.2 Port of Shipment and Port of Destination

The clause concerning the port of shipment and port of destination can be set according to the following instructions:

(1) One port of shipment or destination is generally set in the contract.

(2) Two or more ports of shipment or destination, as the circumstances may require, are stipulated in the contract.

(3) If, at the time of negotiation, the port of shipment or destination is hard to decide, then optional ports can be used. Such as, "CIF London optional", "CIF London/Hamburg/Rotterdam optional" etc. When making such a clause concerning port of shipment or destination, attention should be paid to the following:

Port of shipment or destination in foreign country shall be clearly and definitely stated, and expressions such as "African Main Ports" should not be used. Since "Main Ports" are not clearly defined. In addition, facilities, freight charges and additional freightage differ a great deal from country to country. If, as the circumstances may require, two or more ports are allowed, then these ports chosen should be on the same transportation line and close in distance. Moreover it should be clearly stated in the contract that consequential extra freightage shall be born by the buyer, and that the final port of destination should be announced at the time when the relevant L/C is opened.

5.3.3 Partial Shipment and Transshipment

Partial shipment means making less amount of shipment than what is stated in the letter of credit when only one set of transport documents presented; or making less amount of shipment than what is stated in the letter of credit or using multiple means of conveyance when more than one set of transport documents presented.

Transshipment is the shipment of goods or containers to an intermediate destination, then to yet another destination. One possible reason for transshipment is to change the means of transport during the journey (e. g. , from ship transport to road transport), known as transloading. Another reason is to combine small shipments into a large shipment (consolidation), dividing the large shipment at the other end (deconsolidation). Transshipment usually takes place in transport hubs. Much international transshipment also takes place in designated customs areas, thus avoiding the need for customs checks or duties, otherwise a major hindrance for efficient transport. An item handled (from the shipper's point of view) as a single movement is not generally considered transshipped, even if it changes from one mode of transport to another at several points. Previously, it was often not distinguished from transloading, since each leg of such a trip was typically handled by a different shipper. Transshipment is normally fully legal and an everyday part of world trade. However, it can also be a method used to disguise intent, as is the case with illegal logging, smuggling, or grey-market goods.

Partial shipment is not regulated under cash in advance payment, open account or documentary collections rules. Letter of credit rules have special articles covering partial shipments. Disallowing partial shipments may huge impact on exporter's shipment flexibility, as a result it must be used very carefully. If letter of credit amount cannot be shipped in a single truck and requires more than one truck usage, partial shipment should not be prohibited when road transportation will be used.

Transshipment is not regulated under cash in advance payment, open account or documentary collections rules. Letter of credit rules have special articles covering transshipments. Air transportation mostly requires couple of transshipments before the cargo arrives to the airport of destination. Prohibiting transshipment in air transportation may result undesired consequences. Multimodal transportation must require at least one transshipment.

5.3.4 Shipping Advice

Letter or form sent by an exporter to a foreign buyer informing that the shipment of the ordered goods is on its way. A copy of the invoice and the packing slip (and sometimes a copy of bill of lading) may also be attached. Also called advice note.

The usual practice of international trade under a FOB term is for the seller, if having got ready for shipment, to send a notice to the buyer before the agreed shipment date (usually 30 – 45 days before the shipment date) so that the buyer can arrange the relevant vessel for taking the delivery. The buyer, after receiving the relevant notice by the seller, should at the agreed time, notify the seller of the name of the vessel and the estimated arrival date of the vessel. And the seller, after the goods is placed on board the vessel, should, at agreed time, notify the buyer of the contract number, the name and weight of the goods, the invoice amount, the vessel's name and the date of shipment so that the buyer can make necessary arrangements for purchasing the relevant insurance and taking delivery of the goods.

5.4 Sample Letters

REF: INTRODUCTION LETTER

We are pleased to introduce our reputation in logistics and consequently request you to appoint us your Clearing & Forwarding Agent.

As premier service international Freight Forwarders, we rank second to none in designing logistics infrastructures which provide the best compromise between cost, speed and reliability. This process of designing and executing these logistics plans has earned for the Benairs Logistics the title: "Architect of Transport".

The target groups of Benairs Logistics are those customers for which the standard service of the common forwarding Agents, Airlines and Integrators is not sufficient. We seek to distinguish ourselves by providing the most possible flexibility and reliability in customer service. Our global agency network enable clients to benefit from a package tailored to their individual needs and time requirements.

As an accredited intermediary in your logistics chain, we keep the promise you gave to your customers: JUST-IN-TIME. Attached herewith is an outline of our company's profile, services and rates quotation respectively.

Thank you in advance for your anticipated response.

Yours faithfully,

Managing Director.

COMPANY PROFILE

Mr. Ben Kyalo founded Benairs Logistics Ltd on the 20th Dec 2000. Simultaneously an office was opened at the Jomo Kenyatta International Airport to carry out all forwarding operations. The director attended Trans-Eastern Airlines Aviation College, the FIATA Airfreight Institute (Geneva, Switzerland) and the IATA Training & Development Institute (Montreal, Canada) whereby he graduated with Masters in IATA/FIATA Aviation cargo covering the principles and practices for processing international Airfreight and the IATA Dangerous Goods Regulations respectively.

The director acquired wide knowledge and experience within long years of working for the international forwarding businesses and Airlines; having thereby occupied leading positions. Over the years, the company successfully acquired a highly satisfied number of customers. To consolidate and cultivate confidence in Benairs Logistics, competence is therefore the primary ambition of the company. Benairs Logistics renders the following services in her capacity as IATA cargo Agent/consolidator:

LOGISTICS CHAIN

(a) Going global—a growing trend

Global sourcing is becoming increasingly popular as a way of accessing new opportunities and strengthening your competitive edge. It is common practice for companies to develop a product in the U. S. A, manufacture it in Japan and sell it in Europe. This means that merchandise will often make a longer and perhaps more complicated journey from its source to the final destination—from concept to consumption.

(b) Managing the process

Benairs Logistics chain management services are designed to ensure that each step of your logistics chain is carefully coordinated and managed. Our staff is comprised of professionals who are committed to securing the process so as to meet your requirements. Given our network of agents and logistics partners around the globe, we are in a position to support your buying, selling and logistics processes anywhere in the world.

(c) Linking up with you

In order to better understand your specific needs and expectations, we work closely together with you. We begin by designating a dedicated client team with the exclusive task of examining each step in your logistics chain. Their job is to understand the nature of your business and assist in optimizing your logistics processes. Working in conjunction with you, the client team will develop, implement and maintain standard operating procedures that will suit your specific needs, thus becoming the fundamental document upon which we will operate your logistics chain.

AIRFREIGHT

(a) Timing is everything

Where time is of essence for certain shipments, airfreight is the natural choice. Benairs Logistics understands why valuable time must not be lost. Our highly skilled employees care about your merchandise as much as you do. Processing and overseeing each detail of every stage, so your merchandise arrives safely and as quickly as possible. That includes processing all the administration work, handling and documentation before and after the flight in accordance with the IATA/ICAO regulations. We know that customer success and satisfaction stems not only from our solutions, but also from our staff. Our commercial service team includes international business experts who have in-depth knowledge of global trade as well as our solutions. They are highly trained and experienced in industry standard methodologies.

(b) Elimination of guesswork

To monitor the exact progress of your merchandise through each step, you'll appreciate our global data processing and sophisticated communication network. These Benairs Logistics systems have been designed to make the entire process totally transparent. That way you can make decisions based on real facts and real time. Knowing exactly where your merchandise is—any where, at any time will eliminate the guesswork on your part.

AIR CARGO CHARTERS

At Benairs Logistics, we understand that the punctual, safe and cost-effective delivery of all your air cargo consignments is a fundamental aim of any freight organization. Whatever your shipment, urgent, high value or outsize cargo, our commitment to you is to provide the best solution for all your cargo aircraft chartering needs ranging from Full to Split Charter-flights. Our comprehensive database of all types of aircraft is constantly updated with current locations and availability. Using this knowledge, we aim to provide our clients with the right aircraft at the right time and at the best price to meet all your freight requirements.

The benefits to you:

* We provide a 24 hour, 366 days a year service, ensuring a total commitment to our customers.

* Our expert knowledge combined with our comprehensive freight aircraft database means you get the optimum solution to all your freight requirements.

* Our staff has extensive operational experience and is able to provide effective support and advice at every stage of the operation.

CONSOLIDATION

This is by far the most popular and cost-effective way to effect freight movement. It is based on set flights during the course of the week where the allocation of space is prebooked with the nominated Airline. The freight charge is cheaper than on a direct Master Air Waybill and it also means that flight details can be given quickly. We facilitate our customers by making cargo consolidation by Air/Sea which includes the transportation of cargo to the stuffing point, stuffing the cargo into the container, processing shipping documents with customs, use of premium Air/ Shipping lines and make sure that the cargo will reach the respective destination well before the stipulated time given by the reputed customer. We follow carefully all the important shipping instructions given and take care of your cargo by warehousing it until the shipment will be physically effected.

SEAFREIGHT

Sea freight is an eminent feature among the services offered by Benairs Logistics. Our network of agents and logistics partners worldwide enable our clients to benefit from a package tailored to their individual needs and time requirements. We excel in facilitating our clients with the following Sea freight services:

* Worldwide export consolidation services.
* Import de-consolidation services.
* Handling FCL's/LCL's shipments to worldwide destinations.

FCL: If a shipper/importer has enough cargo to make either a 20ft or 40ft container cost-effective, the product is sold at a container rate. The customer pays an agreed price for the container, it is then totally at his discretion as to how much cargo is placed inside the container—the more tonnage placed inside the container the lower the unit price.

LCL: This is the same type of product, as the consolidation service on airfreight where there is not enough cargo for the shippers needs to warrant paying for a 20ft container. So space is sold at the applicable weight/measure price to and from the major ports throughout the world—this is effectively a group age service.

As we work with all shipping lines, a detailed schedule of services can be provided which high lights the frequency, transit time and real freight costs as they do vary considerably for different lines within the same trade route.

Exercise

I. Multiple Choices

1. The different modes of transportation are ________.

A. road transportation

B. air transportation

C. water transportation

D. rail transportation

2. The characteristics of liner transport are that ________.

A. its freight is determined by the market

B. the line, the port, the time and the freight rate are fixed

C. the obligations and rights of both seller and buyer are stipulated in the B/L

D. the variety and quantity of goods shipped are more flexible

3. ________ is the most important mode of transport in international trade.

A. Sea transport

B. Road transport

C. Air transport

D. Container

4. Which of the following statement is not true about bill of lading? ________

A. You must prepare and submit a Shipper's Letter of Instructions form to your freight forwarder so that they can issue an accurate bill of lading.

B. Bills of lading are one of three crucial documents used in international trade to ensure that exporters receive payment and importers receive the merchandise.

C. Depending on how fast you want to get cargo to your customer and how much he or she is willing to spend, you might ship by ocean or air.

D. A bill of lading is a document issued by a seller to acknowledge receipt of cargo for shipment.

5. Partial shipment may be necessary when ________.

A. direct liners are not available

B. the amount of the cargo is very small

C. the shipping date is very close

D. the export covers a large amount of goods

II. True or False

1. In International trade, a trader has the choice of many different forms of transport by land, sea, or air. ( )

2. Nowadays, air transport is the most important mode of transport in international trade. ( )

3. There are many different kinds of ships, which can be divided into two main groups: tramp vessels and liners. ( )

4. Liners are often used when Bulk carriers and some cruise ships are built. ( )

5. The freight of liners is relatively fixed, while the freight of tramps is mainly determined by the market. ( )

6. Bills of lading are one of three crucial documents used in international trade to ensure that exporters receive payment and importers receive the merchandise. ( )

7. Airway bills serve functions similar to those of ocean bills of lading, but they are only issued in negotiable form. ( )

8. Port of shipment or destination in foreign country shall be clearly and definitely stated, and expressions such as "African Main Ports" can be used. ( )

9. Transshipment means making less amount of shipment than what is stated in the letter of credit when only one set of transport documents presented. ( )

10. Partial shipment means that the goods under one contract are shipped in different terms or by different lots. ( )

III. Questions

1. In international trade, what are the main modes of transportation?

2. Among those different modes of transportation, which mode is most widely used?

3. In sea transportation, what are the difference between tramp vessels and liners?

4. In international trade, what are the main documents in a contract during the imports and exports?

5. "Shipment within 45 days after the receipt of the relevant L/C" is the clause correct? Why or why not?

Chapter Six　Marine Cargo Insurance

This part covers the following topics:

6.1　What Is Insurance;

6.2　What Is Marine Cargo Insurance;

6.3　Insurance Clauses in Sales and Purchasing Contract.

By the end of this part, you will be able to master:

1. The meaning of insurance;
2. The principles of insurance;
3. The classification of risks, coverage and policies in marine cargo insurance;
4. The scope of FPA, WPA, AR, general additional risk and special additional risks;
5. The factors that decide the amount of premium;
6. The insurance clauses according to a particular situation.

6.1　What Is Insurance

6.1.1　Definition of Insurance

Insurance is a means of protection from financial loss. It is a form of risk management primarily used to hedge against the risk of a contingent, uncertain loss. An entity which provides insurance is known as an insurer, insurance company, or insurance carrier. A person or entity who buys insurance is known as an insured or policyholder. The insurance transaction involves the insured assuming a guaranteed and known relatively small loss in the form of payment to the insurer in exchange for the insurer's promise to compensate the insured in the event of a covered loss. The loss may or may not be financial, but it must be reducible to financial terms, and must involve something in which the insured has an insurable interest established by ownership, possession, or preexisting relationship.

The insured receives a contract, called the insurance policy, which details the conditions and circumstances under which the insured will be financially compensated. The amount of money charged by the insurer to the insured for the coverage set forth in the insurance policy is called the premium. If the insured experiences a loss which is potentially covered by the insurance policy, the insured submits a claim to the insurer for processing by a claims adjuster.

6.1.2 Characteristics of Insurance

Insurance involves pooling funds from many insured entities (known as exposures) to pay for the losses that some may incur. The insured entities are therefore protected from risk for a fee, with the fee being dependent upon the frequency and severity of the event occurring. In order to be an insurable risk, the risk insured against must meet certain characteristics. Insurance as a financial intermediary is a commercial enterprise and a major part of the financial services industry, but individual entities can also self-insure through saving money for possible future losses. Risk which can be insured by private companies typically shares seven common characteristics.

Large number of similar exposure units: Since insurance operates through pooling resources, the majority of insurance policies are provided for individual members of large classes, allowing insurers to benefit from the law of large numbers in which predicted losses are similar to the actual losses. Exceptions include Lloyd's of London, which is famous for insuring the life or health of actors, sports figures, and other famous individuals. However, all exposures will have particular differences, which may lead to different premium rates.

Definite loss: The loss takes place at a known time, in a known place, and from a known cause. The classic example is death of an insured person on a life insurance policy. Fire, automobile accidents, and worker injuries may all easily meet this criterion. Other types of losses may only be definite in theory. Occupational disease, for instance, may involve prolonged exposure to injurious conditions where no specific time, place, or cause is identifiable. Ideally, the time, place, and cause of a loss should be clear enough that a reasonable person, with sufficient information, could objectively verify all three elements.

Accidental loss: The event that constitutes the trigger of a claim should be fortuitous, or at least outside the control of the beneficiary of the insurance. The loss should be pure, in the sense that it results from an event for which there is only the opportunity for cost. Events that contain speculative elements such as ordinary business risks or even purchasing a lottery ticket are generally not considered insurable.

Large loss: The size of the loss must be meaningful from the perspective of the insured. Insurance premiums need to cover both the expected cost of losses, plus the cost of issuing and administering the policy, adjusting losses, and supplying the capital needed to reasonably assure that the insurer will be able to pay claims. For small losses, these latter costs may be several times the size of the expected cost of losses. There is hardly any point in paying such costs unless the protection offered has real value to a buyer.

Affordable premium: If the likelihood of an insured event is so high, or the cost of the event so large, that the resulting premium is large relative to the amount of protection offered, then it is not likely that the insurance will be purchased, even if on offer. Furthermore, as the accounting profession formally recognizes in financial accounting standards, the premium cannot be so large that there is not a reasonable chance of a significant loss to the insurer. If there is no such chance of loss, then the transaction may have the form of insurance, but not the substance (see the U. S. Financial Accounting Standards Board pronouncement number 113: "Accounting and Reporting for Reinsurance of Short-Duration and Long-Duration Contracts").

Calculable loss: There are two elements that must be at least estimable, if not formally calculable: the probability of loss, and the attendant cost. Probability of loss is generally an empirical exercise, while cost has more to do with the ability of a reasonable person in possession of a copy of the insurance policy and a proof of loss associated with a claim presented under that policy to make a reasonably definite and objective evaluation of the amount of the loss recoverable as a result of the claim.

Limited risk of catastrophically large losses: Insurable losses are ideally independent and non-catastrophic, meaning that the losses do not happen all at once and individual losses are not severe enough to bankrupt the insurer; insurers may prefer to limit their exposure to a loss from a single event to some small portion of their capital base. Capital constrains insurers' ability to sell earthquake insurance as well as wind insurance in hurricane zones. In the United States, flood risk is insured by the federal government. In commercial fire insurance, it is possible to find single properties whose total exposed value is well in excess of any individual insurer's capital constraint. Such properties are generally shared among several insurers, or are insured by a single insurer who syndicates the risk into the reinsurance market.

6.2 What Is Marine Cargo Insurance

In international buying and selling of goods, there are a number of risks, which, if they occur, will involve traders in financial losses. For instance cargoes in transit may be damaged due to breakage of packing, clash or fire etc. These hazards, and many others, may be insured against. Insurance is a process for spreading risks, so that the burden of any loss is borne not by the unfortunate individual directly affected but by the total body of persons under consideration. In return for a payment known as a premium paid by the insured, an insurance company will agree to compensate the insured person in the event of losses during the period of insurance. Almost all of the international shipments should be insured against loss and damage.

6.2.1 Concepts of Risks

In marine insurance business, losses arise due to various marine risks. Some risks are insured while some risks are not insured. Before we discuss the different types of marine losses, let us first understand the meaning of the term marine risks.

Marine Risks in connection with cargoes in transit can be classified into two categories: Marine Risks and Extraneous Risks.

(a) Marine Risks are caused by Natural Calamity and Accidents;

(b) Extraneous Risks consist of General Extraneous Risks and Special Extraneous Risks.

Disasters such as tsunami, earth quake or volcanic eruption, lighting and heavy weather fall into the category of Natural Calamity; while fire, explosion, sunk, grounding, collision, missing etc. belong to Accidents. It should be noted that Marine Risks do not include all the risks at sea. For instance, fresh and/or water damage are/is not included in the Marine Risks.

Extraneous Risks are risks that are beyond the coverage of the Marine Risks mainly including General Extraneous Risks and Special Extraneous Risks. General Extraneous Risks include: theft/pilferage, contamination, breakage, sweating and/ or heating, taint of odour, rusting, fresh and/or rain water damage, short-delivery and non-delivery, shortage in weight, clashing etc. Special Extraneous Risks include: war, warlike operations, hostile acts, armed conflicts or piracy capture, seizure, arrest, restraint or detainment etc.

It is very important to have a clear understanding of the above mentioned concepts, since some of the risks are not covered by the relevant insurance. For example, partial losses or damages caused by Natural Calamity are not covered by F. P. A; while Special Extraneous Risks are not in the coverage of All Risks.

6.2.2 Marine Losses

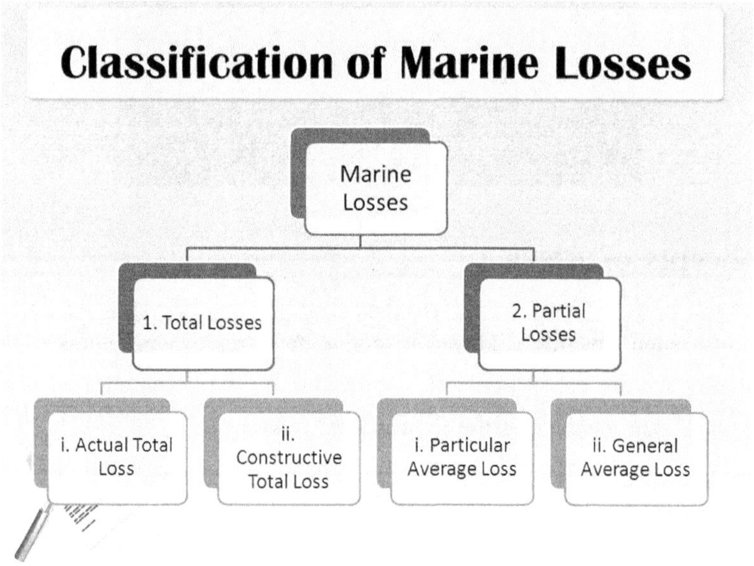

1. Actual total loss and constructive total loss

These two terms are used to differentiate the degree of proof where a vessel or cargo has been lost. An actual total loss occurs where the damages or cost of repair clearly equal or exceed the value of the property. A constructive total loss is a situation where the cost of repairs plus the cost of salvage equal or exceed the value. The use of these terms is contingent on there being property remaining to assess damages, which is not always possible in losses to ships at sea or in total theft situations. In this respect, marine insurance differs from non-marine insurance, where the insured is required to prove his loss. Traditionally, in law, marine insurance was seen as an insurance of "the adventure", with insurers having a stake and an interest in the vessel and/or the cargo rather than simply an interest in the financial consequences of the subject-matter's survival.

The term "constructive total loss" was also used by the United States Navy during World War Ⅱ to describe naval vessels that were damaged to such an extent that they were beyond economical repair. This was most often applied to destroyer-type ships in 1945, the last year of the war, many which were damaged by Kamikazes. By this time enough ships were available for the war that some could be disposed of if severely damaged.

Marine perils are defined as the perils consequent on or incidental to, the navigation of the sea, that is to say, perils of the seas, fire, war perils (enemies), pirates, rovers, thieves, captures, seizures, restraints and detainment of princess and peoples, jettison, barratry and other perils, either of the like kind or which may be designed by thc policy.

Marine losses can be divided into: total losses and partial losses. Total losses include actual total losses and constructive total losses; partial losses consist of general average and particular average. Constructive Total Loss refers to the loss where an accrual total loss appears to be unavoidable or the cost to be incurred in recovering or reconditioning the goods together with the forwarding cost to the destination name in the policy would exceed their value on arrival.

The above said definition discloses the various types of marine perils. They are as follows:

2. Perils of the sea

They refer to all risks, perils and dangers peculiar to the sea. They include accidents, capture of the ship or its cargo by pirates, losses by collision, etc. A point to note here is that losses caused by perils of the sea cannot be prevented by any reasonable care, skill and diligence on the part of human beings.

Thus, if a ship hits a sunken rock and sinks or collides with another ship and suffers a loss, it is a case of loss by perils of the sea. Other examples of such loss are:

(a) Loss of cargo as a result of sea water entering the ship through a hole made by rats in the bottom of the ship.

(b) Loss resulting from negligent navigation, provided it was caused by a peril of the sea.

(c) Loss of cargo due to heat produced by the closing of ventilators to prevent the entry of sea water on rough weather.

3. Fire

Fire is one of the most common perils of the sea and the underwriter is liable for loss caused by it. Though every type of fire is not covered by the policy, damage caused by smoke or by the heat of fire or damage by water used to put out or prevent the spread of fire or fire resulting from lightning, spontaneous combustion, explosion, negligence of the master or crew etc. , are covered by the policy.

If the loss is caused by the wilful misconduct of the insured or the fire takes place on account of the inherent vice or nature of the subject matter insured, the insurer is not responsible. It is to be remembered that certain losses on account of perils of fire not covered by the standard form can be covered by having special clauses and paying the extra charges.

4. Enemies

Enemy literally means one who tries or wishes to harm or attack or one who has ill feeling or hatred towards another. It includes all damages or losses sustained owing to the hostile acts of an enemy. Enemies include all types of ships belonging to the foe or enemy countries and to their hostile acts, provided such acts formed part of the enemy campaign.

5. Jettison

Jettisoning is the voluntary and intentional throwing overboard or away a part of the cargo or part of vessel's equipment for the purpose of lightening or relieving the ship in case of necessity or emergency to have a safe adventure or voyage.

If the cargo or any other thing is thrown overboard accidentally or fortuitously, then it does not constitute jettison. It should, however, be remembered that no jettison of cargo owing to its inherent vice is covered by the policy. For example, the jettison of fruits which have become rotten on account of delay or of hemp shipped in an improper condition which as a result has become dangerously heated, is not covered.

6. Barratry

It refers to every wrongful act willfully committed by the master or crew to the prejudice of the owner without the connivance of the owner. L. J. Scrution defines barratry as any wilful act or wrong doing by the master against ship and goods even though with the intention of benefiting ship owner. Barratry of marines include fraud or crime causing loss or damage to goods committed under circumstances that would not be prevented with the shipowner. Negligence even amounting to recklessness or carelessness will not consistent barratry: there must be an intention to injure vessel or goods. Instances of barratry include running or making away with the ship, willfully carrying her out of the nominated course, sinking or deserting her, embezzling the cargo, smuggling or any other act by which vessel or cargo is subjected to arrest, detention, loss or forfeiture. In the case of "Scuttling", connivance of the owner does not constitute barratry.

7. Men-of-war

It refers to vessels authorized and maintained by nations for the purpose of defense or attack in the event of hostilities and the loss arising out of collision against a man-of-war is covered in a policy.

8. Pirates, rovers, thieves

In the olden days, when means of communications and transport were not so developed, the perils on account of pirates (it means sea robbers but it includes passengers of the ship who rise in revolt or those who attack the ship from the shore), rovers (wanderers and pirates on the high seas), and thieves (robbers using force for violence and not clandestine thieves or pilferers or pick pockets from among the passengers or crew) were very common.

The acts by those persons are committed for the pursuit of private ends by robbery or marauders plundering indiscriminately in places beyond the jurisdiction of a state. In the modern time, however these cases are rare.

9. Restraints

The prevention to free use of a port by the government of the country is known as restraint. It may cause interruption and possible loss of voyages involving such ports and sacrifice of cargo.

10. Detainment

It covers losses due to detention of a vessel and its cargo by blockage or possibly quarantine regulation or other interference by the police of a nation while a vessel is in port. It does not cover losses which are the result merely of delay or interruption of the voyage or loss of market or some other remote result.

11. Arrest

It means forcibly taking away of the vessel and refers to political or executive acts.

12. Letter of mart

It means power granted by a state government to individual citizen who undertakes to attack an enemies merchant ship in revenge for losses where they had themselves suffered.

13. Letter of counter mart

It refers to the power granted by the opposing nation to other persons to resist and retaliate such attacks.

14. Taking at sea

It refers to stopping and taking into port a ship for examination in the event of any suspicion of carrying contraband goods.

6.2.3 Expenses in Reducing Loss

Expenses include a) sue and labor expense; and b) salvage charges. The labor refer to the expenses arising from measures properly taken by the insured, the employee and the assignee etc. for minimizing or avoiding losses caused by the risks covered in the insurance policy; while the latter refer to expenses arising from measures properly taken by a third party other than the insured, the employee and the assignee etc. expenditure incurred by the parties to the adventure on account of salvage, whether under contract or otherwise, shall be allowed in general average to the extent that the salvage operations were undertaken for the purpose of preserving from peril the property involved in the common maritime adventure.

6.2.4 Types of Coverage

According to People's Insurance Company of China Ocean Marine Cargo Clauses, the insurance is mainly classified into two groups: Basic Insurance Coverage and Additional Insurance Coverage. The applicant can purchase Basic Insurance Coverage individually, but he or she cannot purchase Additional Insurance Coverage individually. Before he purchases an Additional Insurance Coverage, he has to purchase a Basic Insurance Coverage.

Basic insurance Coverage is divided into the following three Conditions: Free from Particular Average (F. P. A.), with Particular Average (W. P. A.) and All Risks. F. P. A. does not cover partial losses and expenses that are caused by Natural Calamity. Aside from the risks covered under F. P. A. condition as above, W. P. A. also covers partial losses of the insured goods caused by heavy weather, lightning, earthquake and/or flood. Besides the risks covered under the F. P. A. and W. P. A. conditions above, All Risks also cover all risks of loss of or damage to the insured goods whether partial or total, arising from external causes in the course of transit.

6.2.5 Notes

When effecting insurance with the insurance company it is advantageous for the insurance applicant to bear in mind that:

(1) He or she should avoid duplication coverage of insurance. For instance, it is not right to effect insurance covering All Risks plus Risk of Odour, since Risk of Odour falls into the category of General Extraneous Risks which are actually covered by All Risks.

(2) He or she should purchase one Basic Insurance Condition before he purchases an Additional Risks. For instance, he should purchase a F. P. A. before he purchases the insurance for the coverage of Fresh Water Rain Damage.

(3) The insured must have insurable interest in the subject of insurance.

(4) Not all losses or expenses are covered by the Basic Insurance Condition. For instance, the following losses and expenses shall be excluded from the Basic Insurance Condition:

(a) Loss or damage caused by the intentional act or fault of the insured.

(b) Loss or damage falling under the liability of the consignor.

(c) Loss or damage arising from the inferior quality or shortage of the insured goods prior to the attachment of this insurance.

(d) Loss or damage arising from normal loss, inherent vice or nature of the insured goods, loss of market and/or delay in transit and any expenses arising therefrom.

(5) The insured should present the following documents for making claims against the Insurance Company: Original Policy, Bill of Lading, Invoice, Packing List, Tally Sheet, Weight Memo, Certificate of Loss or Damage and/or Shortage Memo, Survey Report, Statement of Claim. If any third party is involved, documents relative to pursuing of recovery from such party should also be included.

(6) According to the relevant stipulations of the PICC, the validity of a claim shall not exceed a period of two years counting from the time of completion of discharge of the insured goods from the seagoing vessel at the final port of discharge.

6.3 Sample Letters

6.3.1 Sample Letter (1)

Marine Cargo Insurance Claim Letter

To: The Director Recovery
ISL Insurance Ltd. UK

Sir, with due respect, I beg to state that I am a client of your company for the past decade. Insurance is one of my top priorities. By the grace of God, I haven't had any incident which may have propelled me to make any sort of insurance claim up till now. As you know that I am a fond of sea. I have already insured all of my collection. I was away for a business meeting last week and someone stole my boat named "Sea Reaper". Therefore, I am writing this letter to make an insurance claim for that boat. I hope you will take an action on this very soon.

Thank you.
Yours sincerely,
Darwin Margot

6.3.2 Sample Letter (2)

Insurance Claim Letter for Loss

LEAVE A COMMENT
Insurance Claim Letter for Machinery
To: Mr. Liam Payne
Director Claims
IGH Insurance
Nevada, USA

Sir, I am Jackson Abraham and I am a client at your company for over a decade. I opted to require services for my business' insurance for which I have been paying an insurance premium timely. Sadly, there has been an incident at the factory recently. Due to some technical and electrical fault, the mixing machine burnt out resulting in burning the sheets and ruining the whole batch as well. I wish to appeal for insurance claim for the above mentioned loss estimating to MYM 50,000. I hope this matter is taken in notice seriously and promptly.

Yours sincerely,
Jackson Abraham
Datt Town, Houston
Texas, USA

6.3.3 Sample Letter (3)

Office Closing Reason for Business Loss Letter

The Employees
Sobia Zahra BoutiqueLahore
Subject: Closure of the DHA outlet of Sobia Zahra

Dear Employees,
I regret to inform you that our outlet of Sobia Zahra at commercial area DHA is permanently closing down as we have suffered great irrecoverable business losses over the past 2 years. All the taxes and bills against our outlet have been cleared and notices have been put up for the sale of this property. We are sorry to notify that your job here terminates in one month i. e. on 31st August, 2015. You are advised to hunt for new jobs or apply at our other outlets of our company. We express our deepest gratitude to all our employees for their dedicated services at our outlet.

Regards,
Mr. Zaeem Ullah Khan
Branch Manager
Sobia Zahra Boutique

6.3.4 Sample Letter (4)

Placing Transportation Carrier(s) on Notice of a Claim

On your official company letterhead
Date
Name & address of transportation carrier
(ocean, air &/or inland)

To whom it may concern:
We hereby provide you with our Notice of Claim regarding the following matter:
Vessel: ________________
Bill(s) of Lading #: ________________
Container(s)#: ________________

Port of loading: ________________
Port of destination: ________________
Place of delivery: ________________
Shipment: ________________
Shipper: ________________
Consignee: ________________

Statement of Claim
...... (short paragraph describing the damage(s) sustained to the cargo)......
We hold you responsible for the loss sustained and hereby declare that we reserve the right to file a claim with you when the full extent of the claim is ascertained.
Please return a signed copy of this notice to us acknowledging its receipt and advise us within 14 days if you require to inspect the damaged cargo.

Thank you for your cooperation.
Title, name and signature.

Exercises

I. Multiple Choice

1. ________ is a process for spreading risks, so that the burden of any loss is borne not by the unfortunate individual directly affected but by the total body of persons under consideration.

A. Insurance　　B. Trade
C. Transportation　　D. Premium

2. The losses done to the goods in marine transportation can be classified into two types, namely ________.

A. general average and particular average
B. total loss and partial loss
C. basic loss and additional loss
D. actual total loss and constructive total loss

3. In the marine cargo insurance, general average is ________.

A. a kind of partial loss
B. a kind of total loss
C. a partial loss or total loss decide by the time
D. constructive total loss

4. WPA was covered for an exporting goods, and part of the goods was damaged because of the rain on the way, then the insurance company should ________.

A. compensate for none
B. compensate for the whole lot

C. compensate for the part damaged

D. compensate for all the exporting goods

5. The following statements are correct about the marine risks except for ________.

A. earth quake or volcanic eruption, lighting and heavy weather fall into the category of Natural Calamity

B. fire, explosion, sunk, grounding, collision, missing etc. belong to Accidents

C. Marine Risks include all the risks at sea

D. fresh and/or water damage are/ is not included in the Marine Risks

II. True or False

1. A person or entity who sells insurance is known as an insured or policyholder. ( )

2. The amount of money charged by the insurer to the insured for the coverage set forth in the insurance policy is called the premium. ( )

3. Insurance as a financial intermediary is a commercial enterprise and a major part of the financial services industry, and individual entities cannot self-insure through saving money for possible future losses. ( )

4. In marine insurance business, losses arise due to various marine risks. ( )

5. Marine Risks in connection with cargoes in transit can be classified into two categories: Marine Risks and Extraneous Risks. ( )

6. Marine Risks include all the risks at sea. For instance, fresh and/or water damage are/ is not included in the Marine Risks. ( )

7. Extraneous Risks consist of General Extraneous Risks and All Risks. ( )

8. In international trade, if All Risks was covered, any loss caused by any reason on the way can be compensated by insurance company. ( )

9. Special Extraneous Risks are in the coverage of All Risks. ( )

10. Marine Losses can be divided into: Total Losses and Partial Losses. ( )

11. Total Losses include actual Total Losses and Constructive Total Losses; Partial Losses consist of General Average and Particular Average. ( )

III. Questions

1. What is insurance?

2. What are the characteristics of insurance?

3. How many kinds of Marine risks? What are they?

4. What does General Extraneous Risks include?

5. According to People's Insurance Company of China Ocean Marine Cargo Clauses, what is the insurance mainly classified?

Chapter Seven Order and Contract

This part covers the following topics:

7.1 General Terms and Conditions of Contract;

7.2 Order;

7.3 Purchase Contract.

By the end of this part, you will be able to master:

1. General terms and conditions of contract;
2. Order form;
3. Purchase contract form;
4. Letters on orders and contracts.

7.1 General Terms and Conditions of Contract

GENERAL TERMS AND CONDITIONS OF CONTRACT

DATED

CONTRACT NAME

by and between

PARTY A NAME

and

PARTY B NAME

TABLE OF CONTENT

PRELIMINARY STATEMENT

1. DEFINITIONS
2. [OPERATIVE CLAUSES]
3. CONDITIONS PRECEDENT
4. REPRESENTATIONS AND WARRANTIES
5. TERM
6. TERMINATION
7. CONFIDENTIALITY
8. BREACH OF CONTRACT
9. FORCE MAJEURE
10. SETTLEMENT OF DISPUTES
11. APPLICABLE LAW

12. MISCELLANEOUS PROVISIONS

This contract is made in [city and province], China on this day of, 20 by and between [Party A name], [Party A entity form] established and existing under the laws of China, with its legal address at [address] (hereinafter referred to as "Party A"), and [Party B name], [Party B entity form] organized and existing under the laws of [Party B] with its legal address at [address] (hereinafter referred to as "Party B"). Party A and Party B shall hereinafter be referred to individually as a "Party" and collectively as the "Parties".

PRELIMINARY STATEMENT

[add background information if appropriate]

After friendly consultations conducted in accordance with the principles of equality and mutual benefit, the Parties have agreed to [describe subject matter of the Contract] in accordance with Applicable laws and the provisions of this Contract.

Now the Parties Hereby Agree as follows:

1. Definitions

Unless the terms or context of this contract otherwise provide, all term used in this Contract shall have the meanings set out in Schedule A hereto.

2. [Operative Clauses]

3. Conditions precedent

4. Representations and Warranties

(1) Each party represents and warrants to the other Party that on the date hereof:

(a) It is [an independent legal person] duly organized, validly existing and in good standing under the laws of the place of its establishment;

(b) It has full authority to enter into this Contract and to perform its obligations hereunder;

(c) It has authorized its representative to sign this Contract and from and after the Effective Date the provisions of this Contract shall be legally binding upon it;

(d) Its execution of this Contract and its performance of its obligations hereunder

(i) will not violate any provision of its business license, articles of incorporation, articles of association or similar organizational documents;

(ii) will not violate any Applicable Law or any governmental authorization or approval; and

(iii) will not violate or result in a default under any contract to which it is a party or to which it is subject;

(e) No lawsuit, arbitration or other legal or governmental proceeding is pending or, to its knowledge, threatened against it that would affect its ability to perform its obligations under this Contract; and

(f) it has disclosed to the other Party all documents issued by and governmental department that may have a material adverse effect on its ability to full perform its obligations under this Contract, and the documents previously provided by it to the other Party do not contain any misstatements or omissions of material facts.

(2) Consequences of Inaccuracy in Representations

If any of the above representations and warranties of a Party are not accurate in all material respects on the date hereof, then such Party shall be in breach of this Contract.

[Add undertakings if appropriate]

5. Term

(1) Term

Subject to the provisions of Article 2, the term of the Contract ("Term") shall be [---] years, commencing on the Effective Date.

(2) Extension

The Term shall expire automatically on the Expiration Date, unless extended for an additional term of [__] years through a written contract signed by the authorized representatives of the Parties at least [sixty (60)] days prior to the Expiration Date.

6. Termination

(1) Termination

(a) This Contract shall terminate upon the expiration of the Term unless extended pursuant to Article(Term).

(b) This Contract may be terminated at any time prior to expiration of the Term by the mutual written contract of the Parties.

(c) At any time prior to the expiration of the Term, a Party ("Notifying Party") may terminate this Contract through notice to the other Party in writing if:

(i) the other Party materially breaches this contract, and such breach is not cured within the Cure Period granted pursuant to Article(Remedies for Breach of Contract); or

(ii) the other Party becomes bankrupt, or is the subject of proceedings for liquidation or dissolution, or ceases to carry on business or becomes unable to pay its debts as they come due; or

(iii) the conditions or consequences of Force Majeure (as hereinafter defined) which have a material adverse effect on the affected Party's ability to perform continue for a period in excess of six (6) months and the Parties have been unable to find an equitable solution pursuant to Article (Consequences of Force Majeure) hereof; or

(iv) a fundamental provision of this Contract (without which one or both of the Parties would not have entered into the Contract) is declared or becomes invalid under Applicable Law.

(v) [insert other conditions triggering termination as appropriate]

(2) Continuing Obligations

The provisions of Article(Termination), Article (Breach of contract) (but only with respect to claims arising prior to the termination hereof or with respect to other continuing obligations), Article(Confidentiality) and Article (Settlement of Disputes) shall survive the termination of this contract.

7. Confidentiality

(1) From time to time prior to and during the term of this Contract either Party ("disclosing") has disclosed or may disclose Confidential Information to the other Party ("Receiving Party"). The receiving Party shall, during the term of this Contract and for [________] years thereafter:

(a) maintain the confidentiality of Confidential Information;

(b) not to use Confidential Information for any purpose other than those specifically set out in this Contract; and

(c) not disclose any such Confidential Information to any person or entity, except to its employees or employees of its Affiliates, its agents, attorneys, accountants and other advisors who need to know such information to perform their responsibilities and who have signed written confidentiality contracts containing terms at least as stringent as the terms provided in this Article.

(2) The provisions of Article above shall not apply to information that:

(a) can be shown to be known by the receiving Party by written records made prior to disclosure by the disclosing Party;

(b) is or becomes public knowledge otherwise than through the receiving Party's breach of this Contract; or

(c) was obtained by the receiving Party from a third party having no obligation of confidentiality with respect to such information.

(3) Each party shall formulate rules and regulations to inform its directors, senior staff, and other employees, and those of their Affiliates of the confidentiality obligation set forth in this Articles.

(4) Upon the expiration or termination of this Contract, [and in any event upon the disclosing Party's request at any time], the receiving Party shall (i) return to the other Party, or at the disclosing Party's direction destroy, all materials (including any copies thereof) embodying the other Party's Confidential Information and (ii) certify in writing to the other Party, within ten days following the other Party's request, that all of such materials have been returned or destroyed.

8. Breach of Contract

(1) Remedies for Breach of Contract

Except as otherwise provided herein, if a Party ("breaching party") fails to perform any of its material obligations under this Contact, then the other Party ("aggrieved party") may at its option:

(a) give written notice to the breaching party describing the nature and scope of the breach and demand that the breaching party cure the breach at its cost within a reasonable time specified in the notice ("Cure Period"); and

(b) if the breaching party fails to cure the breach within the Cure period, then in addition to its other rights under Article. 1(c)(i)(Termination) or Applicable Laws, the aggrieved party may claim direct and foreseeable damages arising from the breach.

(2) Limitation on Liability

Notwithstanding any other provision of this Contract, neither Party shall be liable to the other Party for damages for loss of revenues or profits, loss of goodwill or any indirect or consequential damages in connection with the performance or non-performance of this Contract. The aggregate liability of a Party for all claims for any loss, damage or indemnity whatsoever resulting from such Party's performance or non-performance of this Contract shall in no case exceed United States Dollars (US $) or the RMB equivalent thereof.

9. Force Majeure

(1) Definition of Force Majeure

"Force Majeure" shall mean all events which are beyond the control of the Parties to this Contract, and which are unforeseen, unavoidable or insurmountable, and which prevent total or partial performance by either of the Parties. Such events shall include earthquakes, typhoons, flood, fire, war, strikes, riots, acts of governments, changes in law or the application thereof or any other instances which cannot be foreseen, prevented or controlled, including instances which are accepted as Force Majeure in general international commercial practice.

(2) Consequences of Force Majeure

(a) If an event of Force Majeure occurs, a Party's contractual obligations affected by such an event under this Contract shall be suspended during the period of delay caused by the Force Majeure and shall be automatically extended, without penalty, for a period equal to such suspension.

(b) The Party claiming Force Majeure shall promptly inform the other Parties in writing and shall furnish within [fifteen (15)] days thereafter sufficient proof of the occurrence and duration of such Force Majeure. The Party claiming Force Majeure shall also use all reasonable endeavours to terminate the Force Majeure.

(c) In the event of Force Majeure, the Parties shall immediately consult with each other in order to find an equitable solution and shall use all reasonable endeavours to minimize the consequences of such Force Majeure.

10. Settlement of Disputes

(1) Friendly consultations

In the event of any dispute, controversy or claim (collectively, "dispute") arising out of or relating to this Contract, or the breach, termination or invalidity hereof, the Parties shall attempt in the first instance to resolve such dispute through friendly consultations.

(2) Arbitration

If any dispute is not resolved by friendly consultations within [sixty (60)] days after the date such consultations were first requested by a Party, then any Party may submit the dispute for arbitration in [xxx] before the [xxx Arbitration Centre] in accordance with its rules of arbitration procedure, supplemented by the following:

(a) There shall be one (1) arbitrator appointed by the arbitration body.

(b) The arbitration proceedings shall be conducted in the English language.

(c) The arbitration award shall be final and binding on the Parties, and the Parties agree to be bound thereby and to act accordingly.

(d) All costs of arbitration shall be borne by the Parties as determined by the arbitration tribunal.

(3) Continuing Rights and Obligations

When any dispute occurs and is the subject of friendly consultations or arbitration, the Parties shall continue to exercise their remaining respective rights and fulfill their remaining respective obligations under this Contract, except in respect of those matters under dispute.

(4) Enforcement of Award

Judgment upon any arbitral award may be entered in any court having jurisdiction over the Party against which the award has been rendered, or application may be made to any such court for judicial acceptance of the award and an order of enforcement, as the case may be. In the event of judicial acceptance and an order of enforcement, each Party expressly waives all rights to object thereto, including any defense of sovereign immunity and any other defense based on the fact or allegation that it is an agency or instrumentality of a sovereign state.

(5) Injunctive Relief

Notwithstanding the foregoing, the Parties agree that each Party has the right to seek injunctive or other similar relief in any court of competent jurisdiction in respect of any claims of breach of confidentiality or IPR infringement.

11. Applicable Law

The validity, interpretation and implementation of this Contract shall be governed by the laws of [the People's Republic of China] [another jurisdiction] (without regard to its rules governing conflict of laws).

12. Miscellaneous Provisions

(1) Independent Contractor Relationship

The parties are only establishing an independent contractor relationship with each other by entering into this Contract. Nothing in this Contract shall be construed or implied as:

(a) establishing between the Parties hereto any partnership or any other form of relationship entailing joint liability;

(b) constituting either of the Parties hereto as the agent of the other Party (except with the other Party's prior written consent); or

(c) authorizing either Party to incur any expenses or any other form of obligation on behalf of the other Party (except with the other Party's prior written consent).

(2) Binding Effect

This Contract is made for the benefit of the Parties hereto and their respective lawful successors and assignees and is legally binding on them.

(3) Amendment

This Contract shall not be changed verbally, but only by a written instrument signed by the Parties.

(4) No publicity

The existence of this Contract, as well as its content, shall be held in confidence by both Parties and only disclosed as may be agreed to by both Parties or as may be required to meet securities disclosure or export permit requirements. Neither Party shall make public statements or issue publicity or media releases with regard to this Contract or the relationship between the Parties without the prior written approval of the other Party.

(5) No Solicitation

Neither Party shall directly solicit for employment the other Party's personnel who are engaged in the performance of this Contract, during the Term of this Contract and within one (1) year after the Expiration Date, without the prior written consent of the other Party.

(6) Notices

Any notice or written communication provided for in this Contract by either Party to the other, including but not limited to any and all offers, writings, or notices to be given hereunder, shall be made in [language] by courier service delivered letter or by facsimile [or electronic mail] and confirmed by courier service delivered letter, promptly transmitted or addressed to the appropriate Party. The date of receipt of a notice or communication hereunder shall be the date of delivery confirmed by the courier service in the case of a courier service delivered letter and the next working day after dispatch in the case of a facsimile [or email]. All notices and communications shall be sent to the appropriate address set forth below, until the same is changed by notice given in writing to the other Party.

(7) Waiver

Failure or delay on the part of any of the Parties hereto to exercise a right under this Contract shall not operate as a waiver thereof, nor shall any single or partial exercise of such a right preclude any other future exercise thereof.

(8) Assignability

This Contract may not be assigned in whole or in part by the Party without the prior written consent of the other Party hereto.

(9) Severability

The invalidity of any provision of this Contract shall not affect the validity of any other provision of this Contract.

(10) Entire Agreement

This Contract and the Schedules and annexes hereto constitute the entire agreement between the Parties hereto with respect to the subject matter of this Contract and supersede all prior discussions, negotiations and agreements between them.

(11) Schedules and Annexes

The Schedules and Annexes hereto are made an integral part of this Contract and are equally binding with the main body of the Contract. In the event of any conflict between the terms and provisions of the main body of the Contract and the Schedules or Annexes, the terms and provisions of the main body of this Contract shall prevail.

(12) Language

This Contract is executed in the Chinese language in ( ) originals and in the English language in ( ) originals. Both language versions shall be equally authentic.

IN WITNESS WHEREOF, each of parties hereto has caused this Contract to be executed by its duly authorized representative on the date first set forth above.

[Party A name]	[Party B name]
By:	By:
Name: [Party A rep name]	Name: [Party B rep name]
Title: [Party A rep position]	Title: [Party B rep position]
Nationality: [Chinese]	Nationality: [Party B rep nationality]

7.2 Order

When a customer has decided to purchase a product, he will place an order. An order in foreign trade is defined as "a request by a customer for a company to supply goods or service". It is the result of a counter offer with a positive acceptance. An order letter is important and widely used. When drafting an order letter, you must be very careful, especially with items, quantities and prices, because a minor mistake may mislead the goods or service providers, which may finally result in the failure of a transaction.

Today, many companies provide specially-designed order forms via website. The forms are sometimes enclosed in catalogs, brochures or pamphlets and then sent to potential customers. When a customer wants to place an order, he only needs to fill in the form which is much easier than writing a complete order letter, and more importantly, order forms are effective in avoiding mistakes.

	A	B	C	D	E	F	G
1			Purchase Order				
2	***Seller:***	Nanjing ZhongShan Int'l Trade Co. Ltd				*No. :*	
3	***Buyer:***	SUNSHINE CLOTHING, AUSTRALIA				*Date:*	
4							
5	Item No.	Description	Specification	color	Qty(pcs)	Unit Price	Amount
6							
7							
8							
9							
10							
11							
12							
13							
14							
15							
16							
17							
18							
19							
20							
21	total:						
22	say total:						
23	The above prices are on FOB Shanghai basis.						
24	*Packing:*						
25	*Payment:*						
26	*Delivery:*						
27	*Marks:*						
28	*Remark:*						

Specimen 7 - 1 Order form

Sample Letters

Letter 7 - 1 Order letter

Dear Mr. Thomas,

Re: Fashion lady bags

Further to our resent discussions through email and we-chat, we should like to confirm the following details:

Item No.	Description	Quantity	Unit Price	Amount
CA351	Lady bag Red	1,000pcs	USD2.31	USD2,310.00
CA358	Lady bag Blue	2,000pcs	USD1.22	USD2,440.00
Total		3,000pcs		USD4,750.00

The above prices are on CFR Shanghai basis.

Packing: Each piece is packed in a polybag then 10pcs in a carton.

Payment: By irrevocable documentary letter of credit opened through Bank of China and drawn at sight.

Delivery: As we need the goods urgently, please deliver within 30days after receipt of the order.

CA351/358
SHANGHAI
NO. 1 up

Shipping Marks: On each and every carton, the following shipping mark should be stenciled:

Remark: In addition to the ordinary shipping documents, please also submit Certificate of Origin for the goods.

Yours faithfully

Letter 7 – 2 Acceptance of Order for lady bags

Dear Mr. Smith,
We are very pleased to receive your Order No. 2796 for 3,000pcs fashion lady bags.
We accordingly accept the order and shall arrange delivery as soon as possible.
Hoping the goods will turn out to your entire satisfaction and we may have further orders from you.
Best Regards

7.3 Purchase Contract

PURCHASE CONTRACT

Contract No.
Date:
No.
Concluded at:
The Buyers:
The Seller:

This contract is made by and between the Buyers and the Sellers, whereby the Buyers agree to buy and the Sellers agree to sell the under-mentioned goods on the terms and conditions stated below:

(1) Name of Commodity, Specifications, Country of Origin, Manufacturers, Packing Terms and Shipping Marks	(2) Quantity	(3) Unit Price	(4) Total Amount	(5) Time of Shipment
The heat number, gross and net weight, package number, measurement and the following Shipping Mark shall be stenciled with unfading pigment on each package: Contract No. ------------------ Port of Destination	( )% ------ more or less allowed on each item			Monthly quantity should be delivered in one shipment with no partial shipment allowed

(6) Port of Loading.

(7) Port of Destination.

(8) Terms of Payment: Upon receipt from the Sellers of the advice as to the time and quantity expected ready for shipment, the Buyers shall open, × × days before shipment, with a bank in China, an irrevocable Letter of Credit in favour of the Sellers payable by the documents as stipulated in Clause (9) of this Contract.

(9) Documents: To facilitate the Buyers to check up, all documents shall be made in a version identical to that used in this Contract.

A. B/L marked "freight prepaid" if based on CIF.

B. Invoice; indicating Contract No., Shipping Marks name of carrying vessel, number of the Letter of Credit and shipment number in case of partial shipments.

C. Packing List and/or Weight Memo; indicating Contract No., Shipping Marks, heat number, gross and net weights of each package.

(10) Terms of CIF Delivery: The Sellers shall undertake to ship the contracted goods from the port of loading to the port of destination on a direct liner, with no transshipment allowed.

(11) Advice of Shipment: The Sellers shall, upon completion of loading, advise the Buyers within 24 hours by fax of Contract No., name of commodity, number of packages, gross and net weights, invoice value, name of vessel and loading date.

(12) Insurance: To be covered by the Buyers from the time when the goods have passed the rail of the vessel. For this purpose the Sellers shall advise the Buyers by telex of the particulars as called for in Clause (11) of this Contract. In the event of the Buyers being unable to arrange for insurance in consequence of the Sellers' failure to send the above advice, the Sellers shall be held responsible for all the losses thus sustained by the Buyers.

(13) Inspection and Claims: The Buyers shall have the right to apply to the Import and Export Commodity Inspection Bureau of the People's Republic of China (CCIB)/China Import and Export Commodity Inspection Corporation (CCIC) for inspection after discharge of the goods at the port of destination. Should the quality and/or quantity/weight be found not in conformity with the contract or invoice or quality certificate, the Buyers shall be entitled to lodge claims with the Sellers on the basis of CCIB/CCIC's inspection certificate within 90 days after discharge of the goods at the port of destination, with the exception, however, of those claims for which the shipping company and/or the insurance company are to be held responsible. All expenses incurred on the claim including the inspection fees are to be borne by the Sellers.

(14) Force Majeure: In case of Force Majeure, the Sellers shall not be held responsible for delay in delivery or non-delivery of the goods but shall notify immediately the Buyers by telex and deliver to the Buyers by registered mail a certificate issued by government authorities or chamber of commerce as evidence thereof: If the shipment is delayed over one month as the consequence of the said Force Majeure, the Buyers shall have the right to cancel this Contract. Sellers' inability in obtaining export license shall not be considered as Force Majeure.

(15) Delayed Delivery and Penalty: Should the Sellers fail to effect delivery on time as

stipulated is this Contract owing to causes other than Force Majeure as provided for in Clause (14) of this Contract, the Buyers shall have the right to cancel the relative quantity of the contract. Or, alternatively, the Sellers may, with the Buyers' consent, postpone delivery on payment of penalty to the Buyers. The Buyers may agree to grant the Sellers a grace period of 15 days. Penalty shall be charged at the rate of 1% of the total value for every 10 days, odd days less than 10 days should be counted as 10 days. The total penalty shall be calculated from the 16th day and shall not exceed 5% of the total value of the goods involved.

(16) Arbitration: All disputes in connection with this Contract or the execution thereof shall be settled by friendly negotiation. If no settlement can be reached, the case in dispute shall then be submitted for arbitration to the China International Economic and Trade Arbitration Commission in accordance with its Rules of Arbitration. The decision made by the Commission shall be accepted as final and binding upon both parties. The fees for arbitration shall be borne by the losing party unless otherwise awarded by the Commission.

(17) The Contract is concluded in Chinese and English with equal authentic.

(18) Additional Clause: If any of the above-mentioned Clause(s) is/are inconsistent with the following additional clause(s), the latter shall be taken as authentic.

THE BUYERS: THE SELLERS:

Exercise

I. Multiple Choice

1. This order ________ the sample you sent us on Oct 11.

A. is placed on B. places on

C. is placed at D. places at

2. We have accepted your Order NO. 598. Please open the relevant L/C ________ here two weeks prior to the date of shipment.

A. which must reach B. when must reach

C. it reaches D. that reached

3. We have decided to place a trial order for the following goods ________ the terms stated in your letter.

A. with B. on

C. by D. at

4. After friendly consultations conducted in accordance with the principles of equality and mutual benefit, the Parties have agreed to buy/sell 200 cartons lights ________ Applicable laws and the provisions of this Contract.

A. accordingly B. according to

C. in accordance with D. in accommodation on

5. The Term shall ________ automatically on the Expiration Date.

A. expect B. except

C. excuse D. expire

6. This Contract shall terminate ________ the expiration of the Term.

A. in B. upon

C. of D. with

7. This Contract may be terminated at any time prior to expiration of the Term by ________ of the Parties.

A. the advice B. fax or email

C. the mutual written contract D. the mutual communication

8. The decision made by the Commission shall be accepted as final and ________ upon both parties.

A. terminal B. binding

C. blinding D. ending

9. Following your order ________ 400pcs of electronic toys last year, we are pleased to receive your order No. 357 ________ the same quantity.

A. for, of B. of, of

C. of, for D. with, for

10. The goods are urgently needed. We ________ hope you will deliver them at once.

A. therefore B. so

C. that D. should

II. True or False

1. In a contract, if all representations and warranties of a Party are not accurate in all material respects on the date hereof, the Party shall be in breach of this Contract. ( )

2. "Force Majeure" only includes earthquakes, typhoons, flood, fire, war, strikes, riots, acts of governments in general international commercial practice. ( )

3. An order in foreign trade is defined as "a request by a customer for a company to supply goods or service". ( )

4. Terms of CIF Delivery: the Buyer shall undertake to ship the contracted goods from the port of loading to the port of destination on a direct liner. ( )

5. All purchase contracts need Advices of shipment. ( )

6. There should not be any change after the Buyer and the Seller have signed a Purchase Contract. ( )

7. All contracts should concluded in Chinese and English with equal authentic. ( )

8. Terms and Payment should be discussed by the buyer and the seller before signing a contract. ( )

9. This Contract shall be changed verbally, or by a written instrument signed by the Parties. ( )

10. If the buyer and the seller could not sign a contract, they have terminated their relationship. ( )

III. Questions

1. What the difficult part in a contract? And why?
2. If we have to change some terms of a contract, how shall we do?
3. When placing an order, what shall we pay attention to?
4. If the seller has to delay the delivery, what should he do according the Purchase Contract in this chapter?
5. What the best way to settle disputes?

Chapter Eight Complaints and Claims

This part covers the following topics:

8.1 Complaints;
8.2 Claims;
8.3 Inspection;
8.4 Arbitration;
8.5 Force Majeure.

By the end of this part, you will be able to master:

1. The expression methods of complaints;
2. Claims in different situations and settlements;
3. General expression of inspection, arbitration and Force Majeure.

8.1 Complaints

8.1.1 Introduction of Complaints

Complaints or claims made by one party against another are normal in international trade. On execution of a sales contract, both the seller and the buyer must abide by the terms and conditions of the contract and strictly perform their respective obligations. If one of the parties breaches the contract, the other may run into trouble, or suffer great loss. In this case, the affected party can either request the defaulter to make sure that such things will not happen again which is known as "complaint", or request him to make up his loss according to the relevant provisions of the contract, which is called "claim".

Accuracy is important in business. However, mistakes do happen. Customers may sometimes receive damaged or defective merchandise, be overcharged at wrong prices, receive their ordered goods too late, or not at all. There are lots of reasons that cause customers to complain.

Generally, in international business, a customer may complain about:

- The prices charged may be excessive or not as agreed (an incorrect bill, invoice, or statement/a bill for merchandise ordered but never received);
- The wrong goods may have been delivered (delivery of unordered/incorrect merchandise);
- The quality may have been found unsatisfactory;
- The goods may have been found damaged, short-weight, missing or late (delivery of damaged or defective merchandise).

8.1.2 Formal Complaint Letter Writing Tips

A formal complaint letter is written as a means to communicate in a semi-official manner to concerned authorities and voice your grievance. The content should be brief and precise and the tone of the letter should be formal and polite.

(1) Start by mentioning item/service requested. Mention new item's specifications, location of store from where it was procured, date of purchase and warranty.

(2) Mention defect/damage noticed on delivery of new item or dissatisfaction in service provided.

(3) Mention if you are returning defective/damaged item to the seller along with copy of warranty-card and payment-receipt.

(4) End by requesting concerned authority of the company to replace/repair the item or render proper service and oblige.

Sample Letters

Letter 8 – 1 Complaint for wrong goods delivery

Dear Sirs,

Re: our Order No. 967 lady bags

We have received the goods under our order No. 967 shipper by S. S. "Happy".

Unfortunately when we opened the case No. 1 – 39, we found it contained completely different articles. They are all wallets but not lady bags as we ordered.

As we need the goods to complete deliveries to our own customers, we must ask you to arrange for the dispatch of replacement at once. We attach a list of contents of case No. 1 – 39, and shall be glad if you will check this with our order and the copy of your invoice.

In the meantime, we are holding the above-mentioned case at your disposal. Please let us know what you wish us to do with it.

Yours faithfully

Letter 8 – 2 Reply of complaint for wrong goods delivery

Dear Mr. xxx,

Re: Your order No. 967

Thank you for your letter of... It was with great regret that we heard case No. 1 – 39 did not contain the goods you ordered

On going into the matter, we find that a mistake was indeed made in packing, through a confusion of number, and we have arranged for the right goods to be dispatched to you at once. Relative documents will be mailed as soon as they are ready.

We will appreciate it if you will keep case No. 1 – 39 and contents until called for by the local agents of xxx Ltd. , our forwarding agent, whom we have instructed accordingly.

Please accept our apologies for the trouble caused to you by the mistake.

Yours faithfully

8.2 Claims

8.2.1 Introduction of Claims

Claims as a noun is defined as a demand for something that somebody has a right to or owns. Claim as a verb is defined as to demand attention or to force somebody to give attention. A claim letter, therefore, is a demand from a customer for something that is due or owed, or something that is a correction of a problem.

A claim should be made as quickly as possible for it can be rejected if it is too late. Some companies have a deadline for claims. For example, you may sometimes read "you must make any claim within two weeks of arrival of goods", or, "claims must be made immediately upon delivery".

To get a proper response, a claim letter must be brief and clear. The issues of complaint must be specified or listed, and acceptable solutions to the problem or requested actions must be spelled out or listed unless you are willing to let the company decide what actions they will take.

Types of claim

- claim regarding selling and buying
- claim regarding transportation
- claim regarding insurance

Settlement of claim (for most transactions)

- making a refund
- compensating for direct losses or expenses
- selling the goods at lower price
- replacing the defective goods

8.2.2 Formal Claim Letter Writing Tips

(1) Give a reference, i. e. the order number, and describe the product with necessary details.

(2) Describe the problem clearly and completely, and state firmly that you expect an adjustment, but do not use any threatening language.

(3) Explain what you expect he supplier to do, e. g. substitute the right merchandise for the wrong, improve service, correct the bill, etc.

(4) Conclude your letter with a request for prompt action. It is better to write a request for adjustment positively and courteously than to write it critically and threateningly. Your positive and courteous tone shows your trust in the supplier that once he is aware of the error, he will solve it immediately.

8.2.3 General Clauses on Claims

(1) In case of quality discrepancy, claim should be lodged by the Buyers within xx days after the arrival of the goods at the port of destination, while for quantity discrepancy, claim should be lodged by the Buyers within 15 days after the arrival of the goods at the port of destination. In all cases, claims must be accompanied by Survey Reports of Recognized Public Surveyors agreed to by the Sellers. Should the responsibility of the subject under claim be found to rest on the part of the Sellers, the Sellers shall, within xx days after receipt of the claim, send their reply to the Buyers together with suggestion for settlement.

(2) Any claim by the Buyers on the goods shipped shall be filed within xx days after arrival of the goods at port of destination and by a survey report issued by a surveyor approved by the Sellers. Claims in respect of matters within the responsibility of the insurance company or of the shipping company will not be considered or by the Sellers.

(3) Should the quality, quantity and/or weight be found not in conformity with those stipulated in this Contract, aside from those usual natural changes of quality and weight in transit and losses within the responsibility of the shipping company and /or insurance company, the Buyer shall have the right within xx day after the arrival of the goods at the port of destination, to lodge claims concerning the quality, quantity or weight of the goods, but the Buyer should provide the Seller with the certificates issued by the concerned Inspection and Quarantine Organization.

Sample Letters

Letter 8 – 3

Dear Sirs,

Re: Claim for inferior quality

We wish to inform you that the goods under our order No. CL-3876 reached us yesterday.

Unfortunately, on receipt of the goods, we observed that the quality is far below the samples and

the goods are no longer suitable for consumption.
We had them re-inspected immediately by our surveyor, Guangzhou Entry-exit Inspection and Quarantine Bureau. Our experts are of the opinion that it was the inferior material used that caused the quality deterioration. This has caused us a great loss. The loss is compelling us with no other option but to make a claim for a compensation of USD10,000.
Please give this matter your prompt attention.
Yours truly

8.3 Inspection

Commodity inspection is the inspection conducted by an authorized third party to testify whether the quality, quantity, weight, package, etc. are the same as those specified in the contract.

8.3.1 Time and Place of Inspection

(1) The goods are inspected at the factory or at the port of shipment (also shipping quality and weight). Inspection results considered final for the delivery of the goods by the seller. Buyer can re-inspect the goods but the result will not serve as the basis for compensation. This is more favorable to the seller.

(2) The goods are inspected at the port of destination (also landed quality and weight)

Inspection results considered final for the delivery of the goods by the seller. Buyer can claim for compensation in the case of discrepancies. This is more favorable to the buyer.

(3) The goods are inspected at the port of destination and re-inspected by the buyer at the port of destination. Inspection results issued at the port of shipment are used as one of the documents for the seller to settle payment. Inspection results issued at the port of destination serve as the basis for the buyer to claim for compensation in the case of discrepancies. This is favorable to both the seller and the buyer.

8.3.2 Inspection Bodies

(1) Types of Inspection Body

There are governmental inspection bodies and non-governmental inspection bodies. As for governmental inspection bodies, it is owned and supervised by governments. It is specialized in inspection of particular commodities or those subject to mandatory inspection. This type of inspection body includes the Food and Drugs Administration (FDA) in USA, the State Administration for Commodity Inspection (SACI) in China, etc.

As for non-governmental inspection bodies, it is privately owned and enjoys the same legal status. This type of inspection body includes Societe Generable De Surveillance S. A. (SGS) in Swiss, Lloyds Surveyors in Britain, Underwriters Laboratories (UL) in USA, etc.

(2) Tasks of the Inspection Body

The inspection body is to inspect goods for import and export. The statutory inspection is for mandatory inspection, while the non-statutory inspection is made on a random basis. It is to exercise supervision and control over the inspection and to accept the entrustment for surveying services and issue certificates of survey.

(3) Inspection Standards

Standards for Mandatory inspection are subject to the standards as specified in the Law and the Regulations. For others, they are subject to the standards agreed upon in the trade contracts.

If there is contradiction between the standards in the Law and the Regulations and those in the contracts, subject to the higher one.

If the standards are not specified in the Law and the Regulations or in the contract, they are subject to the standards of the manufacturing country, or relevant international standards or the standards designated by the state inspection agency.

(4) Inspection Certificate

It is common to supple the following certificates to make an inspection:

- Inspection Certificate of Quality
- Inspection Certificate of Weight or Quantity
- Inspection Certificate of Value
- Inspection Certificate of Origin
- Sanitary Inspection Certificate
- Veterinary Inspection Certificate
- Disinfection Inspection Certificate
- Inspection Certificate on Damaged Cargo

8.3.3 General Clauses on Inspection

In case the quality, quantity or weight of the goods be found not in conformity with those stipulated in this Contract after re-inspection by the China Commodity Inspection and Quarantine Bureau within 60 days after arrival of the goods at the port of destination, the Buyer shall return the goods to or lodge claims against the Seller for compensation of losses upon the strength of Inspection Certificate issued by the said Bureau, with the exception of those claims for which the insurers of owners of the carrying vessel are liable.

All expenses (including inspection and quarantine fees) and losses arising from the return of the goods or claims should be borne by the Seller.

8.4 Arbitration

8.4.1 Methods of Dispute Settlement

There are usually four methods of dispute settlement. They are negotiation, mediation, arbitration and litigation.

(1) Difference between arbitration and mediation

Arbitration involves an impartial third party, like a less formal court, the arbitrator hears evidence and makes a decision. The decision is final.

Mediation involves an impartial third party. The mediator gives suggestions to the solution of disputes, but they do not reach a solution unless all sides agree.

(2) Difference between arbitration and litigation

- The way to submit arbitration or litigation is different.

Submission of arbitration is to submit to arbitration made on the agreement of both parties in advance.

Submission of litigation is to submit to litigation made unilaterally by one of the parties.

- The appointment of arbitrator or judge is different.

Arbitration is appointed by the parties themselves and the third appointed by the arbitration institution.

Litigation is appointed by the government.

- The effectiveness of an award or verdict is different.

Award on arbitration is final and binding on both parties with no right given to revision before a law court.

Litigation on verdict is not final, ie. if one party refuses, he can retain the right to appeal to a higher court.

Arbitration is simpler, less costly and time-consuming and more flexible, therefore is more favorable in dispute settlement.

8.4.2 Arbitration Procedure

(1) Applying for Arbitration

Application shall be made in written form and include the name address of the claimant and the claimee, the arbitration agreement, the facts of the disputes, the claimant's claim and the facts and evidence of the claim.

Application shall be submitted to the Secretariat of the Arbitration Commission.

The arbitration fee shall be paid in advance to the Arbitration Commission.

(2) Forming Arbitration Tribunal

For sole-arbitrator tribunal, only one arbitrator involved. Both parties jointly appoint or jointly authorize the chairman of the arbitration body to appoint.

For collegiate tribunal, three arbitrators involved. The claimant and claimee each appoint an arbitrators. The third one either be jointly appointed by both parties or appointed by the arbitration body.

(3) Hearing an Arbitration Case

A date for oral hearing shall be fixed in advance. Communicate to the parties concerned 30 (in foreign-related cases) or 15 days (in domestic cases) before the date for oral hearing. The omission of an oral hearing shall be made at the request of the parties or with the consent of the parties; and be approved by the arbitration tribunal.

If the oral hearing is omitted, an award shall be made based on the documents only.

(4) Issuing an Award

Concerning the time for the issuance, for arbitration without oral hearing, it is within 9 months from the date of the formation of arbitration tribunal; for arbitration based on oral hearing, it is within 30 days from the date of the oral hearing.

The date of issuance is the date on which the award becomes effective.

The arbitration award is final and binding upon both parties.

(5) Setting Aside an Award

In case of inconformity in the statutory procedure in the award, for example, no arbitration clause in the contract, or, no subsequent written arbitration agreement included, or, the appointment of an arbitrator or the formation of an arbitration tribunal not in consistent with arbitration rules. The party concerned can apply for setting aside the arbitral award.

(6) Enforcing an Award

If an award is not executed within time limit specified, it can be applied to the competent court for enforcement.

In applying for enforcement, one party shall submit a written application for enforcement, the arbitration agreement and the original copy of arbitral award.

8.4.3 General Clauses on Arbitration

(1) All disputes in connection with this Contract or the execution thereof shall be amicably settled through negotiation. In case no settlement can be reached between the two parties, the case under dispute shall be submitted to the Foreign Trade Arbitration Commission of the China Council for the Promotion of International Trade for arbitration. Arbitration shall take place in Beijing, China and shall be executed in accordance with the Provisional Rules of Procedure of the said commission, and the decision made by the commission shall be accepted as final and binding upon both parties.

(2) If any dispute is not resolved by friendly consultations within [sixty (60)] days after the date such consultations were first requested by a Party, then any Party may submit the dispute for arbitration in [Singapore] before the [Singapore International Arbitration Centre] in accordance with its rules of arbitration procedure, supplemented by the following:

(a) There shall be one (1) arbitrator appointed by the arbitration body.

(b) The arbitration proceedings shall be conducted in the English language.

(c) The arbitration award shall be final and binding on the Parties, and the Parties agree to be bound thereby and to act accordingly.

(d) All costs of arbitration shall be borne by the Parties as determined by the arbitration tribunal.

(3) An arbitration clause shall be regarded as existing independently and separately from the other clauses of the contract.

(4) An arbitration agreement is part of the contract, but existing independently and separately from the other clauses of the contract.

8.5 Force Majeure

8.5.1 Definition of Force Majeure

"Force Majeure" shall mean all events which are beyond the control of the Parties to this Contract, and which are unforeseen, unavoidable or insurmountable, and which prevent total or partial performance by either of the Parties. Such events shall include earthquakes, typhoons, flood, fire, war, strikes, riots, acts of governments, changes in law or the application thereof or any other instances which cannot be foreseen, prevented or controlled, including instances which are accepted as Force Majeure in general international commercial practice.

8.5.2 Consequences of Force Majeure

(1) If an event of Force Majeure occurs, a Party's contractual obligations affected by such an event under this Contract shall be suspended during the period of delay caused by the Force Majeure and shall be automatically extended, without penalty, for a period equal to such suspension.

(2) The Party claiming Force Majeure shall promptly inform the other Parties in writing and shall furnish within [ ] days thereafter sufficient proof of the occurrence and duration of such Force Majeure. The Party claiming Force Majeure shall also use all reasonable endeavors to terminate the Force Majeure.

(3) In the event of Force Majeure, the Parties shall immediately consult with each other in order to find an equitable solution and shall use all reasonable endeavors to minimize the consequences of such Force Majeure.

To be in general, the parties could postpone the contract when the performance of the contract is delayed temporarily. Contract shall be resumed after the force majeure event. Or, the Buyer and the Seller terminate the contract when the performance of contract is impossible. One of the parties who suffers the force majeure event may ask for the termination of the contract.

8.5.3 General Clauses on Force Majeure

The seller shall not be responsible for late delivery or non-delivery of the goods owing to "Force Majeure" causes, such as war, flood, fire, storm, heavy snow, earthquake, seaquake, etc. However, in such cases, the Seller shall immediately notify the Buyer by email or fax about the accident and furnish the Buyer with a certificate attesting such event or events.

Exercise

I. Multiple Choice

1. The analysis of the first shipment is not ________ certified by China Commodity Inspection Bureau.

A. satisfy　　B. satisfied

C. satisfactory　　D. satisfaction

2. Your delay in shipment will ________ us in great difficulty.

A. cause　　B. lead

C. conclude　　D. involve

3. You can file a claim with the insurance company in your area, who will ________ the

loss incurred.

A. compensate B. compensate for

C. compensate to you D. compensate you

4. The ________ between the products and samples is normal, so we could not accept the claim.

A. discrepancy B. mistake

C. wrong D. change

5. ________ the delay on the part of the suppliers, we must ask you to extend the date of shipment from July 11th to August 12th.

A. Owing to B. According to

C. In order to D. So as to

6. Your failure to ________ our invoice within the stipulated time limit will cause us much inconvenience.

A. draw B. withdraw

C. honor D. dishonor

7. We have lodged a claim ________ ABC & Co. ________ the quality of the goods shipped ________ m. v. "Peace".

A. against... for... by B. with... for... under

C. on... against... as per D. to... for... per

8. We are sorry for the short delivery by 20 tons. This ________ you some trouble in meeting orders of your clients.

A. must cause B. must have caused

C. has caused D. will be caused

9. ________ the goods, we discovered that they were overall inferior in quality to the sample.

A. On examination B. After examination

C. Examination of D. Upon examining

10. After inspection of the above shipment we found 6 cases ________.

A. loss B. losing

C. missed D. missing

II. True or False

1. Accuracy is important in business. It is not allowed to have any mistakes. ( )

2. A formal complaint letter should be brief and precise and the tone of the letter should be formal and polite. ( )

3. A claim could be made at any time after the receipt of goods. ( )

4. Inspection results issued at the port of destination serve as the basis for the buyer to claim for compensation in the case of discrepancies. This is favorable to both the seller and the buyer. ( )

5. The inspection body is to inspect goods for Sellers. ( )

6. Arbitration is simpler, less costly and time-consuming and more flexible among four methods of dispute settlement, therefore is more favorable in dispute settlement. ( )

7. Application shall be made in written form and include the name address of the claimant and the claimee, the arbitration agreement, the facts of the disputes, the claimant's claim and the facts and evidence of the claim. ( )

8. In the event of Force Majeure, the Parties shall immediately consult with each other in order to find an equitable solution and shall wait for the consequences of such Force Majeure. ( )

9. If an award for the inspection is not executed within time limit specified, it can be applied to the competent court for enforcement. ( )

10. In a claim letter, please describe the problem clearly and completely, and state firmly that you expect an adjustment, but do not use any threatening language. ( )

III. Questions

1. What is the difference between "complaint" and "claim"?
2. What's the use of an inspection certificate?
3. How to choose the time and place of inspection?
4. Please explain the arbitration procedure.
5. What is Force Majeure? How to settle our goods if we have to face Force Majeure?

Chapter Nine Import and Export Procedures

This part covers the following topics:

9.1 Import Procedures;

9.2 Export Proeedures.

By the end of this part, you will be able to master:

1. Difference between import and export;
2. Procedures of importing and exporting;
3. Parties involved;
4. Documents used in the procedures.

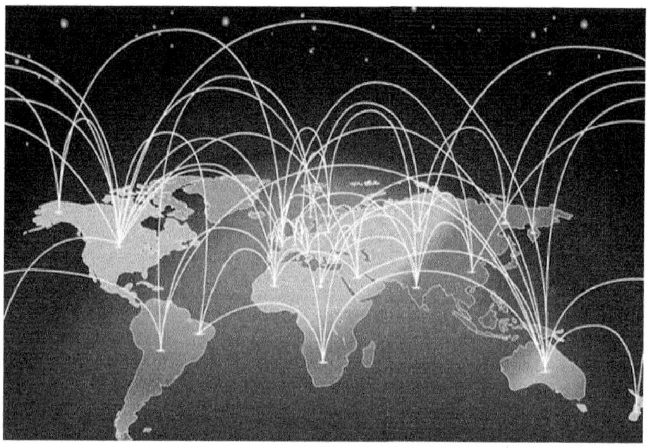

Import and export are terms that are commonly heard in international trade and these activities are carried out by all countries in the world. In general, import refers to an item coming inside a country from any other country while export refers to an item going out of the country to any other country of the world. Since no country in the world is self sufficient, all countries both import as well as export and both exports and imports are essential for the development of any country. Before talking about the import and export procedures, let's review all the parties involved in international trade, see Table 9 – 1.

Table 9 – 1 Parties concerned in international trade

	Parties	Functions
1	importer (buyer, consignee, drawee)	buys or purchases commodities
2	exporter (seller, consignor, drawer)	sells and provides commodities

Table 9 – 1 (Continued)

	Parties	Functions
3	freight forwarder (carrier, forwarding agent)	also known as a non-vessel operating common carrier (NVOCC), organizes shipments for individuals or corporations to get goods from the manufacturer or producer to a market, customer or final point of distribution
4	shipping company	provides transportation services
5	insurance company	provides insurance services for the cargo
6	inspection institution	provides inspection services and issues relevant certificates of inspection
7	customs	approves the import and export of goods
8	banks	provides settlement and finance services to the importer and exporter

9.1 Import Procedures

Procedures in importing can be illustrated by the following Diagram 9 – 1.

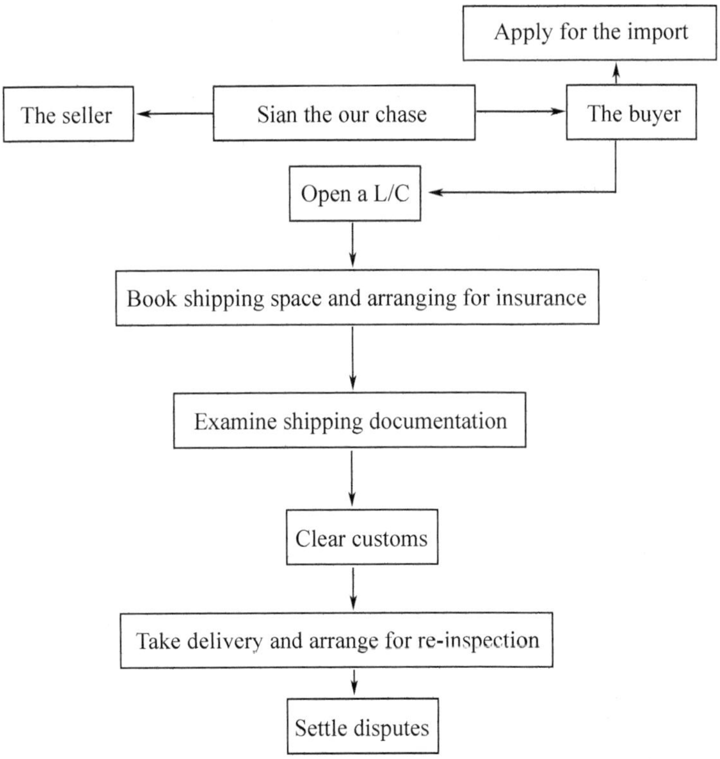

Diagram 9 – 1

9.1.1 Apply for Import License

An import license is a document issued by a national government authorizing the importation of certain goods into its territory. Import licenses are considered to be non-tariff barriers to trade when used as a way to discriminate against another country's goods in order to protect a domestic industry from foreign competition. Each license specifies the volume of imports allowed, and the total volume allowed should not exceed the quota. Government may put certain restrictions on what is imported as well as the amount of imported goods and services.

Before negotiating a contract, the buyer hands in license application and the relevant documents to the relative authority for obtaining the import license. The application form usually includes description of goods, quantity, quantity, unit price and total value, etc.

9.1.2 Open a L/C

A letter of credit is a method of payment that is an important part of international trade. They are particularly useful where the buyer and seller may not know each other personally and are separated by distance, differing laws in each country and different trading customs. It is an assurance given by a buyer's bank as issuing bank to a seller as beneficiary against sale of goods as per the terms and conditions mentioned in Letter of Credit. According to the import contract, if the payment is made by L/C, the buyer should fill in an application form for the issuing of a L/C. Once the issuing bank has ascertained that the applicant will be able to pay for the goods, it will issue the letter of credit. Issuance charges, covering negotiation, reimbursements and other charges are paid by the applicant or as per the terms and conditions of the L/C. If the L/C does not specify charges, they are paid by the applicant.

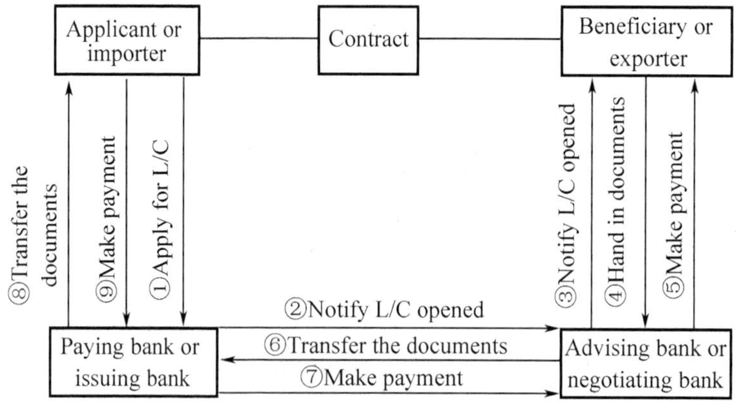

The letter of credit is limited in terms of time, the validity of credit, the last date of shipment, and in terms of how much late after shipment the documents may be presented to the Nominated Bank.

9.1.3 Book Shipping Space and Arranging for Insurance

On the FOB basis, the buyer shall book shipping space in accordance with the date of shipment specified in the contract. Once receiving the estimated time of shipment from the sellers, the buyer should contact the carrier or freighter forwarder to ascertain the shipping matters. After signing the shipping contract, the buyer should inform the seller the name of the vessel, estimated time of arrival to the port of shipment, etc. so that the seller can prepare for shipment.

Insurance is a means of protection from financial loss. It is a form of risk management primarily used to hedge against the risk of a contingent, uncertain loss. Either the exporter or the importer will be liable for the goods at any point in the journey. According to the latest Incoterms 2015, for some terms, the risks of goods have been transferred from the seller to the buyer once the goods have been effectively passed the ship's rail at the port of shipment. Under FOB or CFR terms, the seller must give prompt notice to the buyer right after shipment of goods in order to let the buyer insure the goods without any delay. If the seller fails to give shipping notice to the buyer, the seller will bear any risks or damages owing to that.

9.1.4 Examine Shipping Documentation and Make Payment

The buyer makes payment against right documents. So the examination of seller's documents becomes crucial to the buyer before payment. Under L/C payment, he paying bank examines the documents according to the L/C, and decides whether or not he will make the payment or acceptance against it. If the bank confirms that the documents are correct, he will send them to the importer for further examination. After the importer acknowledges the documents' integrity, the bank will make the payment according to the clauses of L/C. When some unconformity is found, the bank will discuss with the importer. If the importer accepts the unconformity, he can instruct the bank to make payment or acceptance.

9.1.5 Clear Customs

One of the biggest challenges for importers is clearing customs for their products once they arrive into their home country. When the products arrive into the buyer's home country (for example a sea port when arriving via sea), they will not be released to the buyer until the appropriate paperwork is filled out along with paying the necessary duties. When importing goods, almost all countries require, at a minimum, two pieces of paper work: a commercial invoice from your supplier or some official customs forms. A commercial invoice is simply an invoice your supplier will give you, normally before you pay for your goods. It's simply an invoice showing what you're ordering. The official customs form is unique to all countries, and in some countries it's more complex than others. According to different regulations, some related documents are also examined including packing lists, import license etc.

9.1.6 Take Delivery and Arrange for Re-inspection

The buyer presents the B/L to the carrier to take delivery of the goods imported. The quality and quantity of the cargo received by the buyer may not be in conformity with that stipulated in the contract. Hence, the buyer usually applies to Import and Export Commodities Inspection Bureau for the re-inspection of the goods. If the goods are found not complied with the contract, such as shortage in weight, inferior quality or any damage to the goods, the buyer may make claims against the exporter, carrier or insurance company, using the inspection certificate or the surveyor's report as the evidence.

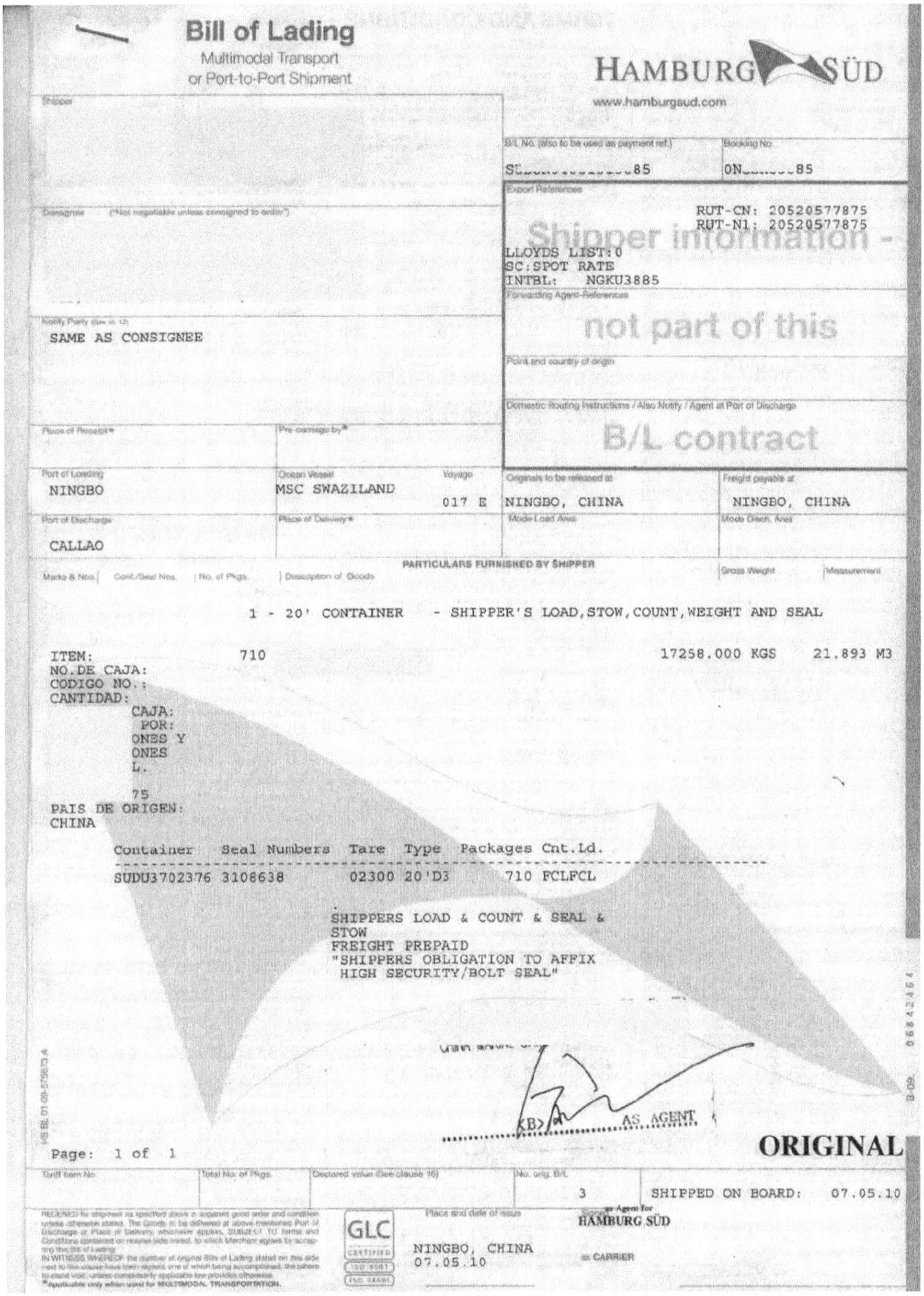

Bill of Lading
Multimodal Transport
or Port-to-Port Shipment

HAMBURG SÜD
www.hamburgsud.com

Shipper

B/L No. (also to be used as payment ref.): SL..........85
Booking No: ON.........85

Export References
RUT-CN: 20520577875
RUT-N1: 20520577875
LLOYDS LIST: 0
SC: SPOT RATE
INTBL: NGKU3885

Consignee (*Not negotiable unless consigned to order*)

Forwarding Agent-References

Notify Party
SAME AS CONSIGNEE

Point and country of origin

Domestic Routing Instructions / Also Notify / Agent at Port of Discharge

Shipper information - not part of this B/L contract

Place of Receipt*	Pre-carriage by*		
Port of Loading: NINGBO	Ocean Vessel: MSC SWAZILAND; Voyage: 017 E	Originals to be released at: NINGBO, CHINA	Freight payable at: NINGBO, CHINA
Port of Discharge: CALLAO	Place of Delivery*	Mode Load Area	Mode Disch. Area

PARTICULARS FURNISHED BY SHIPPER

Marks & Nos.	Cont./Seal Nos.	No. of Pkgs.	Description of Goods	Gross Weight	Measurement
			1 - 20' CONTAINER - SHIPPER'S LOAD, STOW, COUNT, WEIGHT AND SEAL		
ITEM: NO. DE CAJA: CODIGO NO.: CANTIDAD: CAJA: POR: ONES Y ONES L. 75 PAIS DE ORIGEN: CHINA		710		17258.000 KGS	21.893 M3

Container	Seal Numbers	Tare	Type	Packages	Cnt. Ld.
SUDU3702376	3108638	02300	20'D3	710	FCLFCL

SHIPPERS LOAD & COUNT & SEAL & STOW
FREIGHT PREPAID
"SHIPPERS OBLIGATION TO AFFIX HIGH SECURITY/BOLT SEAL"

AS AGENT

Page: 1 of 1

ORIGINAL

Tariff Item No.	Total No. of Pkgs.	Declared value (See clause 7)	No. orig. B/L	
			3	SHIPPED ON BOARD: 07.05.10

Place and date of issue: NINGBO, CHINA 07.05.10

as Agent for HAMBURG SÜD as CARRIER

GLC CERTIFIED

9.1.7 Make a Claim and Compensation

When the carrier, the seller or the insurer fails to fulfill his obligations and causes damages or losses to the buyer, claiming for compensation usually happens. The buyer lodges a claim against the seller, the shipping company or the insurance company. Arbitration is an important means of settling a dispute.

9.2 Export Procedures

In China, most of the exports are based on CIF basis with terms of payment by L/C. Besides CIF, FCA, CPT and CIP are also widely in practice. Procedures in exporting can be illustrated by the flow chart on CIF basis, ocean transportation and payment by L/C, see Diagram 9 – 2.

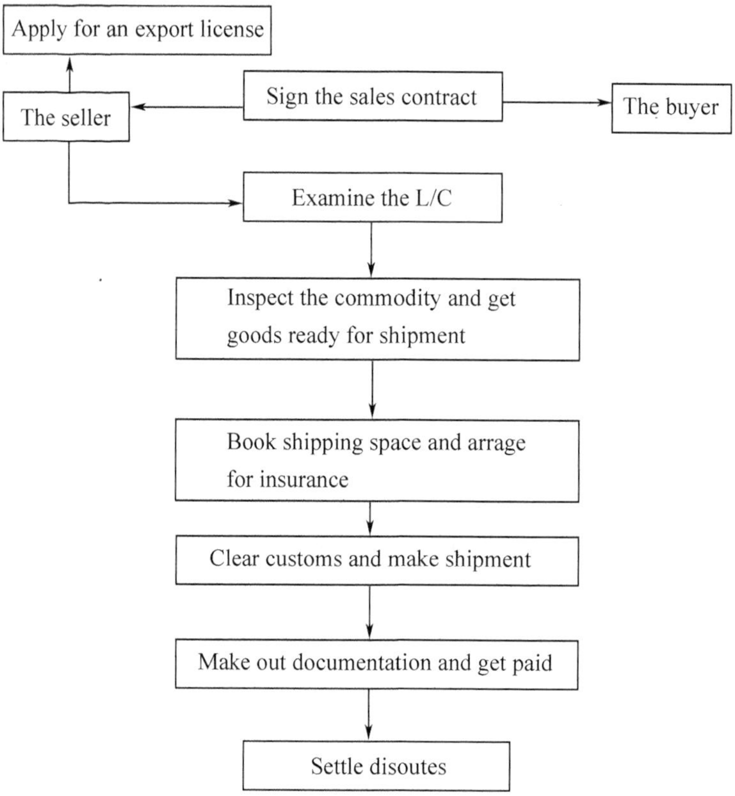

Diagram 9 – 2

9.2.1 Apply for an Export License

In some cases, the seller before negotiating a contract, may need to hand in the relevant documents to the relevant government department in order to apply for an export license. Export license issued by a government agency is to monitor the export of sensitive technologies (such as advanced computer chips, encryption-decryption software), prohibited materials (drugs, genetically-modified plants), dangerous materials (explosives, radioactive substances), strategic materials (uranium, advanced alloys), or goods in short supply in the home market (foodstuffs, raw materials).

9.2.2 Examine the L/C

Typically, after a sales contract has been negotiated and a letter of credit has been agreed upon as the method of payment, the applicant (the buyer) will contact a bank to ask for a letter of credit to be issued. Once the beneficiary (the seller) receives the letter of credit, he will check the terms to ensure that it matches with the contract and will either arrange for shipment of the goods or ask for an amendment to the letter of credit so that it meets with the terms of the contract. Once the issuing bank has ascertained that the applicant will be able to pay for the goods, it will issue the letter of credit.

Once the goods have been shipped, the beneficiary will present the set of requested documents to the Nominated Bank. This bank will check the documents, and if they comply with the terms of the Letter of Credit, the issuing bank is bound to honor the terms of the letter of credit by paying the beneficiary. If the documents do not comply with the terms of the letter of credit they are considered discrepant. At this point the Nominated Bank will inform the Beneficiary of the discrepancy and offer a number of options depending on the circumstances after consent of applicant. If the discrepancies are minor, it may be possible to present corrected documents to the bank to make the presentation compliant. Documents presented after the time limits mentioned in the credit are also considered discrepant.

9.2.3 Inspect the Commodity and Get Goods Ready for Shipment

In order to fulfill a sale contract, the seller must prepare goods according to the time limit stipulated in the contract and in accordance with the latest date of shipment in L/C. Commodity Inspection is one of the important parts in foreign trade. In the process of performing the contract, a series of activities such as delivery, payment, claims and adjustment and so on are based on Certificate of Commodity Inspection. So it plays an important role in foreign trade. The seller applies to the authorized inspection institution to conduct the inspection before shipment. After the inspection of the goods bound for export, the inspection institutions issue inspection certificates.

Before shipment, the buyer sometimes sends his shipping requirements to the seller, informing him in writing of the packing, shipping marks and mode of transport, etc., known as the Shipping Instructions. Packing not only serves as a form of protection, but also facilitates loading, unloading and stowage, and prevents pilferage. Packing should not only be designed to suit shipping requirements but also tally with the regulations in the country of destination. The buyer is under certain conditions entitled to reject the goods if not packed with his instruction or provisions agreed upon.

Shipment is one of the important links in import and export trade. The terms of shipment cover mainly the mode of shipment, time of shipment, port of shipment and port of destination, shipping documents, partial shipment, transshipment, etc. , which should be explicitly stipulated in the contract.

9.2.4 Book Shipping Space and Arranging for Insurance

In international trade, it is a common practice that the exporter books shipping space through shipping companies or the freight forwarder. The freight forwarder goes through all information of shipping including route, schedule, carrier, name of port of call, name and nationality of vessel, etc. As soon as the freight forwarder determines the proper vessel and carrier, he will book shipping spaces with the carrier by submitting booking note. When the carrier confirms the shipping arrangement, stamps on the S/O (shipping order) and returns it to the freight forwarder, the shipping contract between the carrier and freight forwarder becomes effective.

Under CIF term, the seller should insure the goods before they are leaving warehouse or other storage places. After the seller's filling in an application for foreign transportation insurance, the insurer will issue an insurance certificate to the insured as per instructions in the application.

AXA redefining / standards

Winterthur Insurance (Asia) Ltd, Shanghai Branch
11/F, SOUTH TOWER, CHINA DIAMOND EXCHANGE CENTER, NO.1701 CENTURY AVE, PUDONG DISTRICT, SHANGHAI, 200122, CHINA
Tel :(8621) 6156 3500 Fax :(8621) 68824600
Website: www.axa-ins.com.cn

INSURANCE CERTIFICATE

At request of the Insured, Winterthur Insurance (Asia) Ltd. Shanghai Branch (hereinafter called the Company) agrees to issue the insurance certificate as per the Combined General Liability Insurance scheme tailormade for the insured.

TYPE	Combined General Liability Insurance (Public and Products Liability)
POLICY NO.	P0015097
INSURED	ROTAREX STAR ROTAREX International
PRODUCTS	Various valves, fittings, regulators and systems Mainly in gas controlled fields manufactured by ROTAREX STAR & ROTAREX International at its named insured premises.
INSURANCE PERIOD	From January 1 2011 to December 31 2011, both dates inclusive
INDEMNITY LIMIT	EUR1,000,000 any one accident and in aggregate
TERRITORY LIMIT	Worldwide excluding USA/Canada
RETROACTIVE DATE	January 1 2009

The liability of the Company is subject to the terms and conditions of the insurance Policy No. P0015097. Any claims payable will be settled only after the agreed premium is paid by the Insured.

Issuance Date: February 10, 2011

9.2.5 Clear Customs and Make Shipment

Before shipment, the seller should fill in a customs declaration form and submit toe the customs together with copy of the contract, the export license, the commercial invoice, copy of the L/C, the packing list and the shipping order, etc.

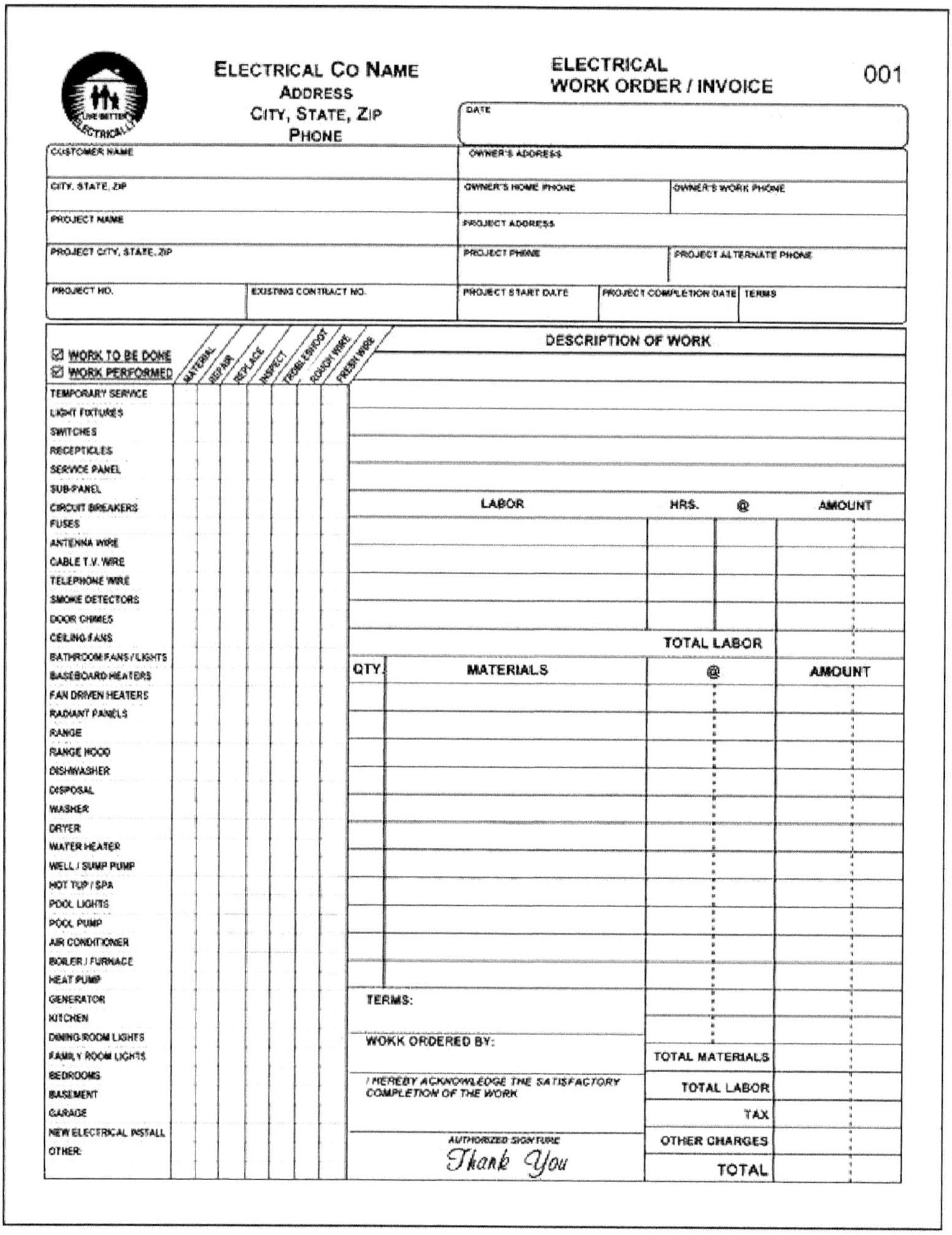

ELECTRICAL CO NAME
ADDRESS
CITY, STATE, ZIP
PHONE

ELECTRICAL
WORK ORDER / INVOICE
001

	DATE
CUSTOMER NAME	OWNER'S ADDRESS
CITY, STATE, ZIP	OWNER'S HOME PHONE / OWNER'S WORK PHONE
PROJECT NAME	PROJECT ADDRESS
PROJECT CITY, STATE, ZIP	PROJECT PHONE / PROJECT ALTERNATE PHONE
PROJECT NO. / EXISTING CONTRACT NO.	PROJECT START DATE / PROJECT COMPLETION DATE / TERMS

☑ WORK TO BE DONE
☑ WORK PERFORMED

	MATERIAL	REPAIR	REPLACE	INSPECT	TROUBLESHOOT	ROUGH WIRE	FRESH WIRE
TEMPORARY SERVICE							
LIGHT FIXTURES							
SWITCHES							
RECEPTICLES							
SERVICE PANEL							
SUB-PANEL							
CIRCUIT BREAKERS							
FUSES							
ANTENNA WIRE							
CABLE T.V. WIRE							
TELEPHONE WIRE							
SMOKE DETECTORS							
DOOR CHIMES							
CEILING FANS							
BATHROOM FANS / LIGHTS							
BASEBOARD HEATERS							
FAN DRIVEN HEATERS							
RADIANT PANELS							
RANGE							
RANGE HOOD							
DISHWASHER							
DISPOSAL							
WASHER							
DRYER							
WATER HEATER							
WELL / SUMP PUMP							
HOT TUP / SPA							
POOL LIGHTS							
POOL PUMP							
AIR CONDITIONER							
BOILER / FURNACE							
HEAT PUMP							
GENERATOR							
KITCHEN							
DINING ROOM LIGHTS							
FAMILY ROOM LIGHTS							
BEDROOMS							
BASEMENT							
GARAGE							
NEW ELECTRICAL INSTALL							
OTHER:							

DESCRIPTION OF WORK

LABOR	HRS.	@	AMOUNT
	TOTAL LABOR		

QTY.	MATERIALS	@	AMOUNT

TERMS:

WORK ORDERED BY:

I HEREBY ACKNOWLEDGE THE SATISFACTORY COMPLETION OF THE WORK

AUTHORIZED SIGNATURE

Thank You

TOTAL MATERIALS	
TOTAL LABOR	
TAX	
OTHER CHARGES	
TOTAL	

After the customs examines the goods, it will sign and seal on the shipping order if the goods are in conformity with the L/C and other legal documents. Thus the goods can be loaded on board the vessel. Meanwhile, the customs will also stamp with "proof seal" on the verifying and writing-off instruments, with which the seller applies for verification at the State Administration of Foreign Exchange (SAFE).

After shipping, the seller will immediately send out the shipping advice to the buyer as per the instruction of the L/C to help the buyer to take out insurance.

9.2.6 Make out Documentation and Get Paid

After shipment, the seller should draw up or prepare all documents according to the terms of L/C strictly, such as Bill of Lading (B/L), Insurance Policy, Inspection Certificate, Bill of Exchange, Commercial Invoice and Packing List ect. which must be correct, complete, concise and clear. Then the seller presents all documents to the bank in the seller's place, often named the negotiating bank. The negotiating bank negotiates the documents and pays funds to the beneficiary in accordance with the L/C. Then the issuing bank credits the negotiating bank's account, if issuing bank checks the documents error free.

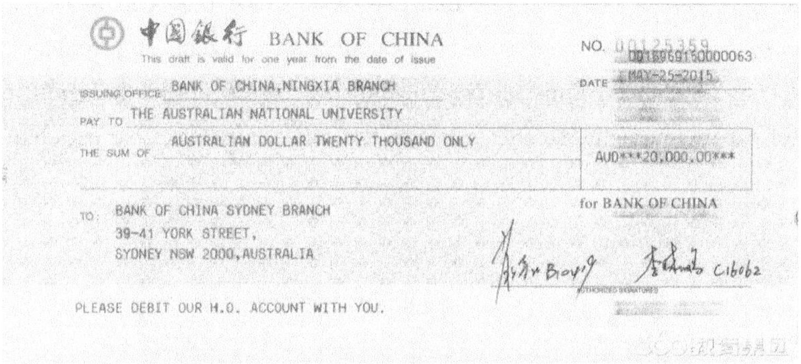
中国银行 BANK OF CHINA
This draft is valid for one year from the date of issue

NO. 00125359
DATE MAY-25-2015

ISSUING OFFICE BANK OF CHINA,NINGXIA BRANCH
PAY TO THE AUSTRALIAN NATIONAL UNIVERSITY
THE SUM OF AUSTRALIAN DOLLAR TWENTY THOUSAND ONLY | AUD***20,000.00***

TO: BANK OF CHINA SYDNEY BRANCH
39-41 YORK STREET,
SYDNEY NSW 2000,AUSTRALIA

for BANK OF CHINA

PLEASE DEBIT OUR H.O. ACCOUNT WITH YOU.

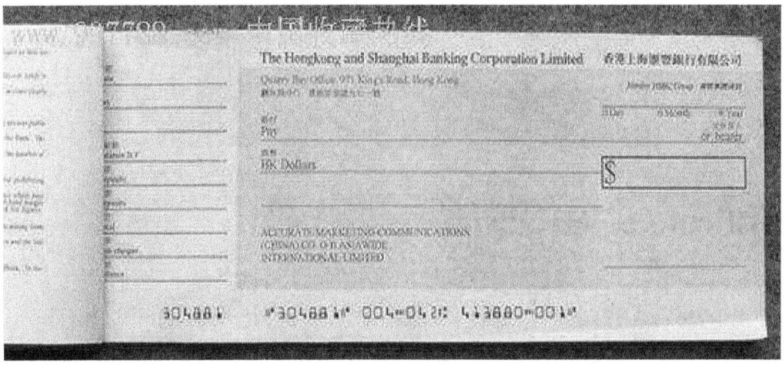

9.2.7 Settle Disputes

Disputes are occasionally found in business and likely to be caused by different reasons such as inferior quality, less quantity, poor or wrong packing, delay in shipment, discrepancy between the samples and the goods actually arrived etc. Once disputes arise, the seller must take it seriously to find out the party to whom the claims are against and evidence of claims within valid time. As for dispute settlements, conciliation is better than arbitration, and arbitration is better than litigation.

9.3 Main Documents

There are a great variety of documents that may need to be produced to complete import and export transactions, such as transport documents, administrative documents, commercial documents, and insurance documents. Some estimates indicate 200 different documents are used in foreign trade. However, in most export transactions, only a few certain documents are used as follows.

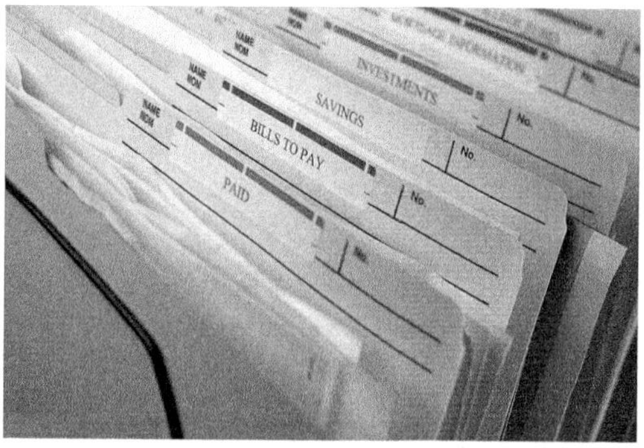

9.3.1 Certificate of Origin

A certificate of origin (often abbreviated to C/O or CoO) is a document used in international trade. In a printed form or as an electronic document, it is completed by the exporter and certified by a recognized issuing body, attesting that the goods in a particular export shipment have been produced, manufactured or processed in a particular country. A "Certificate of Origin" is also called a "Form A".

9.3.2 Import and Export License

If your business is considering exporting or importing goods, you will need to check if you need a license. It is a government document that authorizes the import and export of specific goods in specific quantities to a particular destination. The requirements to gain an import-export license typically vary based on specified criteria, such as the items being imported-exported and where the products are being imported-exported.

9.3.3 Commercial Invoice

A commercial invoice is the core accounting document describing the commercial transaction made by the seller in the name of the buyer. When used in foreign trade, a commercial invoice is a customs document. It is used as a customs declaration provided by the person or corporation that is exporting an item across international borders. Although there is no standard format, the document must include a few specific pieces of information such as the parties involved in the shipping transaction, the goods being transported, the country of manufacture, and the Harmonized System codes for those goods. All the contents of it should be strictly in accordance with that in the contract and L/C.

9.3.4 Packing List

A packing list is a shipping document that accompanies delivery packages, usually inside an attached shipping pouch or inside the package itself. It commonly includes an itemized detail of the package contents and does not include customer pricing. It varies depending on the business and its products and serves to inform all parties, including transport agencies, government authorities, and customers, about the contents of the package. Many receivers use the packing list as a guide or checklist when unpacking their order. If something is missing from the box, they cross-check it with the packing list and then alert the seller.

9.3.5 Inspection Certificate

An inspection certificate is a document certifying that the commodity what you are shipping is, in fact, what the customer has ordered, and is also in good condition at the time of inspection, usually immediately prior to shipment. The requirement is likely to arise from the customer's wish. When used as a required document under L/C terms, the details and identity of the party providing the inspection should be mentioned. An inspection certificate can be furnished directly to a buyer, a buyer's government or direct to a buyer's bank. In the case of presenting to a buyer's bank, that is precipitated by the request of a Letter of Credit payment transaction that spells out specifically an inspection certificate is required in order to fulfill payment obligations.

9.3.6 Insurance Policy or Certificate

It is necessary in shipping of commodities. The insurance policy or certificate is issued by an insurance company, which certifies that an insurance policy or certificate has been bought and shows an abstract of the most important provisions of the insurance contract. But it is not a substitute for the actual policy, and is normally a non-negotiable document. It cannot be assigned to a third party, and is unacceptable under the terms of a letter of credit and in making a claim. In marine insurance (where cargo is insured against a floating insurance policy), it serves to assure the consignee that insurance is in effect for the goods in transit and a proper policy will follow.

9.3.7 Bill of Lading

A bill of lading (sometimes abbreviated as B/L or BoL) is a document issued by a carrier (or his agent) to acknowledge receipt of cargo for shipment. In British English, the term relates to ship transport only, and in American English, to any type of transportation of goods. A bill of lading must be negotiable, and serves the following three main functions:

- it is a conclusive receipt, i. e. an acknowledgement that the goods have been loaded;
- it contains or evidences the terms of the contract;
- it serves as a document of title of goods, which means anyone who gets the bill of lading owns the batch of goods.

The bill of lading is one of three crucial documents used in international trade to ensure that exporters receive payment and importers receive the merchandise.

9.3.8 Bill of Exchange

A bill of exchange is a legally binding, written document that orders a certain party to pay a specific amount of money to a second party. Some bills of exchange may say that the money is due on a predetermined future date, or they may state that payment is due on demand.

It's used in the transaction of goods and services. The bill of exchange is signed by the party that owes money (the payer) and given to the party entitled to the money (the seller or payee), who can then use it to fulfill a contract for payment. However, the seller may also endorse the bill of exchange and transfer it to someone else, thereby passing the payment on to another party.

Note that when a bill of exchange is issued by a financial institution, it's often called a bank draft. When it's issued by an individual during a transaction, it's referred to as a trade draft.

Exercise

I. Multiple Choice

1. In international trade, one party usually has different names, which of the following is not the role of the buyer? ________.

A. Applicant　　B. Importer

C. Consignee　　D. Payee

2. Certificate of Origin is ________.

A. a bill of exchange at sight　　B. the city of original goods

C. a document issued by an authority　　D. a shipping list

3. Under CIF term, the insurance should be covered by ________.

A. the buyer
B. the buyer's agent
C. the seller
D. the seller's agent

4. Which is not the correct settlement for business disputes? ________.

A. Debates
B. Arbitration
C. Conciliation
D. Litigation

5. Which of the following documents shows the title of goods? ________.

A. Packing list
B. Bill of lading
C. Import license
D. Commercial invoice

II. True or False

1. Every country in the world both imports and exports because no country in the world can be self sufficient. ( )

2. The seller needs to book shipping space and arranging for insurance, so does the buyer in some circumstances. ( )

3. It is only the exporter who should examine the L/C. ( )

4. A commercial invoice is the key accounting document for import and export. ( )

5. The L/C can be corrected directly by applicant and be transferred to the beneficiary. ( )

6. The seller often books shipping space by himself for it is his responsibility. ( )

7. When the L/C is verified, the accordance between documents and L/C and between documents and documents is necessary. ( )

8. The buyers have the right to re-inspect the quality and weight of goods after the goods arrived at the port of destination. If the commodity is not acceptable, all expenses (including inspection fees) and losses arising from the return of the goods or claims will be charged by the sellers. ( )

9. After making shipment, the seller should, no matter on what trade terms the transaction is concluded, promptly advise the buyer. ( )

10. If there is any damage or loss to the goods, the buyer can only lodge a claim against the carrier. ( )

III. Questions

1. Suppose you are an importer, could you briefly describe the main procedures in importing?

2. Suppose you are an exporter, could you briefly describe the main procedures in exporting?

3. What is the difference between import and export?

4. List the necessary documents involved in international trade.

5. When using L/C as the method of payment, what's the important aspect we should notice?

Chapter Ten Trade Protectionism

This part covers the following topics:

10.1 Trade Agreements and Business Entities;

10.2 Business Entity;

10.3 Trade Protectionism.

By the end of this part, you will be able to master:

1. Elements of trade agreements;
2. Advantages and disadvantages of assorted trade agreements;
3. The definition of business entity;
4. Forms of business entity;
5. Trade protectionism;
6. The forms of trade protectionism;
7. Advantages and disadvantages of trade protectionism;
8. Solutions to occurring problems.

10.1 Trade Agreements and Business Entities

Trade agreements are when two or more nations agree on the terms of trade between them. They determine the tariffs and duties that countries impose on imports and exports. All trade agreements affect international trade.

10.1.1 Three Types of Trade Agreements

There are three types of trade agreements. The first is a unilateral trade agreement. It occurs when a country imposes trade restrictions and no other country reciprocates. A country can also unilaterally loosen trade restrictions, but that rarely happens. It would put the country at a competitive disadvantage. The United States and other developed countries only do this as a type of foreign aid. They want to help emerging markets strengthen certain industries. The foreign industry is too small to be a threat. It helps the emerging market's economy grow, creating new markets for U. S. exporters.

Bilateral trade agreements are between two countries. Both countries agree to loosen trade restrictions to expand business opportunities between them. They lower tariffs and confer preferred trade status with each other. The sticking point usually centers around key protected or subsidized domestic industries. For most countries, these are in the automotive, oil or food production industries. The United States has 16 bilateral agreements. The Obama administration was negotiating the world's largest bilateral agreement. It was the Transatlantic Trade and Investment Partnership with the European Union.

Multilateral trade agreements are the most difficult to negotiate. These are among three countries or more. The greater the number of participants, the more difficult the negotiations are. They are also more complex, since each country has its own needs and requests.

Once negotiated, multilateral agreements are very powerful. They cover a larger geographic area. That confers a greater competitive advantage on the signatories. All countries also give each other most favored nation status. They agree to treat each other equally.

The largest multilateral agreement is the North American Free Trade Agreement. It is between the United States, Canada and Mexico. Their combined economic output is MYM 20 trillion. NAFTA quadrupled trade to MYM 1.14 trillion in 2015. But it also cost between 500,000 to 750,000 U. S. jobs. Most were in the manufacturing industry in California, New York, Michigan and Texas. The United States has one other multilateral regional trade agreement. The United States negotiated the Central American-Dominican Republic Free Trade Agreement. It was with Costa Rica, Dominican Republic, Guatemala, Honduras, Nicaragua and El Salvador. It eliminated tariffs on more than 80 percent of U. S. exports.

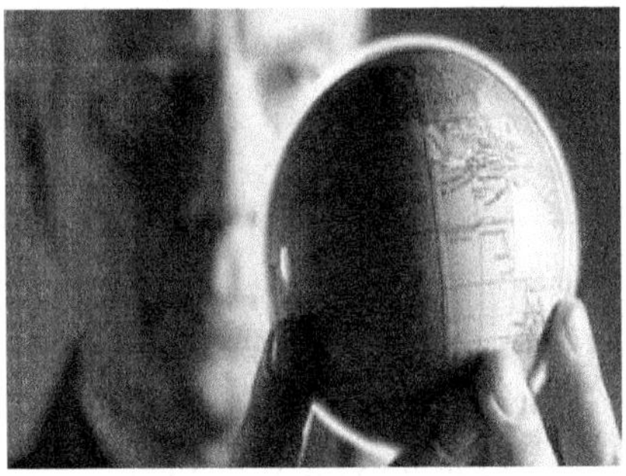

10.1.2 Free Trade Agreements

Free trade agreements reduce or eliminate tariffs and quotas between trading partners. The largest agreement is the NAFTA. It is between the United States, Canada and Mexico. If approved, two other agreements would be larger: the Trans-Pacific Partnership and the Transatlantic Trade and Investment Partnership.

Another free trade agreement is the Dominican Republic-Central America Free Trade Agreement, which is between the United States and Central America. There are also bilateral agreements with Chile, Colombia, Panama, Peru, Uruguay, most countries in Southeast Asia and the Middle Eastern countries of Israel, Jordan, Morocco, Bahrain and Oman. But FTAs don't eliminate protectionist measures like subsidies or currency wars. One of the disadvantages of NAFTA was that subsidized U. S. farm products put Mexican farmers out of business.

10.1.3 Advantages of Free Trade Agreements

Free trade agreements are designed to increase trade between two countries. Increased trade has six main advantages:

(1) Increased economic growth. It is reported that the U. S. Trade Representative Office estimates that NAFTA increased U. S. economic growth by 0.5 percent a year.

(2) More dynamic business climate. Often, businesses were protected before the agreement. These local industries risked becoming stagnant and non-competitive on the global market. With the protection removed, they have the motivation to become true global competitors.

(3) Lower government spending. Many governments subsidize local industry segments. After the trade agreement removes subsidies, those funds can be put to better use.

(4) Foreign direct investment. Investors will flock to the country. This adds capital to expand local industries and boost domestic businesses. It also brings in U. S. dollars to many formerly isolated countries.

(5) Expertise. Global companies have more expertise than domestic companies to develop local resources. That's especially true in mining, oil drilling and manufacturing. Free trade agreements allow the global firms access to these business opportunities. When the multi-nationals partner with local firms to develop the resources, they train them on the best practices. That gives local firms access to these new methods.

(6) Technology transfer. Local companies also receive access to the latest technologies from their multinational partners. As local economies grow, so do job opportunities. Multi-national companies provide job training to local employees.

10.1.4 Disadvantages of Free Trade Agreements

The biggest criticism of free trade agreements is that they are responsible for job outsourcing.

There are seven total disadvantages:

(1) Increased job outsourcing. Why does that happen? Reducing tariffs on imports allows companies to expand to other countries. Without tariffs, imports from countries with a low cost of living cost less. It makes it difficult for U. S. companies in those same industries to compete, so they may reduce their workforce. Many U. S. manufacturing industries did, in fact, lay off workers as a result of NAFTA. One of the biggest criticisms of NAFTA is that it sent jobs to Mexico.

(2) Theft of intellectual property. Many developing countries don't have laws to protect patents, inventions and new processes. The laws they do have aren't always strictly enforced. As a result, corporations often have their ideas stolen. They must then compete with lower-priced domestic knock-offs.

(3) Crowd out domestic industries. Many emerging markets are traditional economies that rely on farming for most employment. These small family farms can't compete with subsidized agri-businesses in the developed countries. As a result, they lose their farms and must look for work in the cities. This aggravates unemployment, crime and poverty.

(4) Poor working conditions. Multi-national companies may outsource jobs to emerging market countries without adequate labor protections. As a result, women and children are often subjected to grueling factory jobs in sub-standard conditions.

(5) Degradation of natural resources. Emerging market countries often don't have many environmental protections. Free trade leads to depletion of timber, minerals and other natural resources. Deforestation and strip-mining reduce their jungles and fields to wastelands.

(6) Destruction of native cultures. As development moves into isolated areas, indigenous cultures can be destroyed. Local peoples are uprooted. Many suffer disease and death when their resources are polluted.

(7) Reduced tax revenue. Many smaller countries struggle to replace revenue lost from import tariffs and fees.

10.1.5 Multilateral Trade Agreements

Multilateral trade agreements are commerce treaties between three or more nations. The agreements reduce tariffs and make it easier for businesses to import and export. Since they are among many countries, they are difficult to negotiate.

That same broad scope makes them more robust than other types of trade agreements once all parties sign. Bilateral agreements are easier to negotiate but these are only between two countries. They don't have as big an impact on economic growth as does a multilateral agreement.

10.1.6 Benefits of Multilateral Agreements

Multilateral agreements make all signatories treat each other the same. That means no country can give better trade deals to one country than it does to another. That levels the playing field. It's especially critical for emerging market countries. Many of them are smaller in size, making them less competitive. See more on the benefits of the Most Favored Nation Status.

The second benefit is that it increases trade for every participant. Their companies enjoy low tariffs. That makes their exports cheaper.

The third benefit is it standardizes commerce regulations for all the trade partners. Companies save legal costs since they follow the same rules for each country.

The fourth benefit is that countries can negotiate trade deals with more than one country at a time. Trade agreements undergo a detailed approval process. Most countries would prefer to get one agreement ratified covering many countries at once.

The fifth benefit applies to emerging markets. Bilateral trade agreements tend to favor the country with the best economy. That puts the weaker nation at a disadvantage. But making emerging markets stronger helps the developed economy over time. As those emerging markets become developed, their middle class population increases. That creates new affluent customers for everyone.

10.1.7 Disadvantages of Multilateral Agreements

The biggest disadvantage of multilateral agreements is that they are complex. That makes them difficult and time-consuming to negotiate. Sometimes the length of negotiation means it won't take place at all.

Second, the details of the negotiations are particular to trade and business practices. That means the public often misunderstands them. As a result, they receive lots of press, controversy and protests.

The third disadvantage is common to any trade agreement. Some companies and regions of the country suffer when trade borders disappear. Smaller businesses can't compete with giant multi-nationals. They often lay off workers to cut costs. Others move their factories to countries with a lower standard of living. If a region depended on that industry, it would experience high unemployment rates. That makes multilateral agreements unpopular.

10.1.8 The Role of the WTO in Trade Agreements

Once agreements move beyond the regional level, they usually need help. The World Trade Organization steps in at that point. It is an international body that helps negotiate global trade agreements. Once in place, the WTO enforces the agreements and responds to complaints. The WTO currently enforces the General Agreement on Tariffs and Trade. The world almost received greater free trade from the next round, known as the Doha Round Trade Agreement. If successful, Doha would have reduced tariffs across the board for all WTO members.

Unfortunately, the two most powerful economies refused to budge on a key sticking point. Both the United States and the EU resisted lowering farm subsidies. These subsidies made their food export prices lower than those in many emerging market countries. Low food prices would have put many local farmers out of business. When that happens, they must look for jobs in overcrowded urban areas. The U. S. and EU refusals to cut subsidies doomed the Doha round. It is a thorn in the side of all future world multilateral trade agreements.

The failure of Doha allowed China to gain a global trade foothold. It has signed bilateral trade agreements with dozens of countries in Africa, Asia and Latin America. Chinese companies receive rights to develop the country's oil and other commodities. In return, China provides loans and technical or business support.

10.2 Business Entity

A business entity is an entity that is formed and administered as per corporate law in order to engage in business activities, charitable work, or other activities allowable. Most often, business entities are formed to sell a product or a service. There are many types of business entities defined in the legal systems of various countries. These include corporations, cooperatives, partnerships, sole traders, limited liability company and other specifically permitted and labelled types of entities. The specific rules vary by country and by state or province. Some of these types are listed below, by country. For guidance, approximate equivalents in the company law of English-speaking countries are given in most cases.

10.2.1 Various Functions of Business Entities

The various functions of business entities can be grouped into the following broad categories:
Production Function;
Marketing Function;
Finance Function;
Human Resource Function;

Management Information Function;
Innovation (Research & Development).

1. Production function

Production is the creation of goods and services with the help of certain processes. The production of goods depends essentially on the organisation of men, money, materials, and facilities into a smoothly operating business. In modern organisations, production is highly organised, mechanized, and specialised mass production, and, therefore, its overall charge is entrusted to the Production Manager.

A production manager has four basic responsibilities in this regard: (i) to ensure the production of goods and services in specified quantities, (ii) to meet the specified time schedule or delivery dates, (iii) to fulfill the quantity requirements, and (iv) to perform all production operations at the minimum cost.

In order to fulfill these responsibilities, the production manager has to perform a number of functions, such as production planning, production engineering (concerned with design of tools, jigs, and installation or equipment), plant layout, plant building, materials handling, purchasing, inventory management, work improvement and work measurement, production control, and the maintenance of physical environment of production.

2. Marketing function

Marketing is the process of getting goods and services into the hands of the consumer with a view to satisfying the needs and desires of consumers and producers. In other words, the marketing function creates a process through which producers and consumers are brought together in an exchange relationship and transfer of ownership takes place.

For this, the marketing manager must make judicious decisions regarding 4 P's: (i) product (decisions about new product development, packaging, branding, etc.); (ii) physical distribution (decisions about marketing channels, and policies and procedures relating to warehousing, transportation, etc.); (iii) promotion (involving advertising, salesmanship, sales promotion, and publicity); and (iv) pricing (policies and procedures relating to the setting up of profitable prices).

3. Finance function

Finance function of business is basically responsible for three decisions and their proper implementation, such as investment decisions (financial planning, capital budgeting, etc.), financial decisions (capital structure—fixed and working; short and long-term and dividend decisions).

Business maintains relationship with financial markets including institutions and major shareholders and also takes care of other concerns such as share buybacks, capital raising sources of borrowings and risk management.

4. Human Resource (HR) function

The HR function deals with the human side of business. It is concerned with increasing the effectiveness of human performance in any organization. Specifically stated, the HR function aims at obtaining arid maintaining a capable and effective workforce, motivating the employees individually and in groups to contribute their maximum to the fulfillment of organizational goals.

In order to accomplish the goals of dynamic HR management, the HR manager has to undertake the following functions: selection—determination of manpower requirements, job analysis, nature and sources of recruitment, employee selection, and induction and follow-up; training—human resource development; promotions and transfers, employee compensation—wage and salary administration; employee involvement and welfare activities; and industrial relations—industrial discipline, industrial unrest, trade unionism, and workers'participation in management. For the accomplishment of these functions, the personnel department renders specialised services.

5. Information function

Like production, marketing, finance, and human resource, the information function is equally important in a modern business. It is being increasingly recognized that the modern business cannot be managed without the assistance of efficient information function. The information function is basically concerned with records.

The net result of the preparation of records is the generation of a mass of "information", and therefore, the purpose of information function is to collect, generate, and communicate, in clearly and easily intelligible form the information to all those who need it, especially to executives for purposes of decision making and policy formulation.

Thus, information cell acts as a storehouse of valuable information and real brain behind every activity of a business concern. The responsibility of performing this function should be entrusted to the information manager in the organization because information function is a specialist function requiring an expert knowledge and technical skill in this area of the operation. The scope of information function in a modern business is very wide.

The information manager is generally burdened with the following three broad functions: information function (receiving and collecting, recording and preserving, arranging and analyzing, and providing information); operational function (such as systems and procedures, records management, etc.); and public relations function.

6. Innovation

"An innovation is the implementation of a new or significantly improved product (good or service), or process, a new marketing method, or a new organization method in business practice, workplace organization or external relations." Thus, innovation, which means creativity as well, is more of a philosophy and the entire business function needs to adopt it.

Here in terms of new product development we are talking about Research and Development. In this age of increasing rivalry among competing firms, the importance of innovation is hardly exaggerating. Normally businesses innovate through product or process.

Innovation often is stimulated by creative thinking on the part of people who are willing to think "outside the box".

The above description clearly explains that these functions of business are basic in nature, and mutually dependent. Each has a separate objective and should be so organized and performed that it contributes to the realization of the objectives of the other. This will ultimately help realize the overall objectives of the business. This process of one function realizing its own objectives and also contributing to other' objectives is known as the "End-means Chain".

10.2.2 Corporations

A corporation is a company or group of people authorized to act as a single entity (legally a person) and recognized as such in law. Early incorporated entities were established by charter (i. e. by an ad hoc act granted by a monarch or passed by a parliament or legislature). Most jurisdictions now allow the creation of new corporations through registration. In a general sense, a corporation is a business entity that is given many of the same legal rights as an actual person. Corporations may be made up of a single person or a group of people, known as sole corporations or aggregate corporations, respectively.

Corporations come in many different types but are usually divided by the law of the jurisdiction where they are chartered into two kinds: by whether they can issue stock or not, or by whether they are formed to make a profit or not.

Where local law distinguishes corporations by the ability to issue stock, corporations allowed to do so are referred to as "stock corporations", ownership of the corporation is through stock, and owners of stock are referred to as "stockholders" or "shareholders". Corporations not allowed to issue stock are referred to as "non-stock" corporations; those who are considered the owners of a non-stock corporation are persons (or other entities) who have obtained membership in the corporation and are referred to as a "member" of the corporation.

Corporations chartered in regions where they are distinguished by whether they are allowed to be for profit or not are referred to as "for profit" and "not-for-profit" corporations, respectively.

There is some overlap between stock/non-stock and for-profit/not-for-profit in that not-for-profit corporations are always non-stock as well. A for-profit corporation is almost always a stock corporation, but some for-profit corporations may choose to be non-stock. To simplify the explanation, whenever "Stockholder" or "Shareholder" is used in the rest of this article to refer to a stock corporation, it is presumed to mean the same as "member" for a non-profit corporation or for a profit, non-stock corporation.

Registered corporations have legal personality and are owned by shareholders whose liability is generally limited to their investment. Shareholders do not typically actively manage a corporation; shareholders instead elect or appoint a board of directors to control the corporation in a fiduciary capacity. In most circumstances, a shareholder may also serve as a director or officer of a corporation.

In American English, the word corporation is most often used to describe large business corporations. In British English and in the Commonwealth countries, the term company is more widely used to describe the same sort of entity while the word corporation encompasses all incorporated entities. In American English, the word company can include entities such as partnerships that would not be referred to as companies in British English as they are not a separate legal entity.

Despite not being individual human beings, corporations, as far as US law is concerned, are legal persons, and have many of the same rights and responsibilities as natural persons do. For example, a corporation can own property, and can sue or be sued. Corporations can exercise human rights against real individuals and the state, and they can themselves be responsible for human rights violations.

Corporations can be "dissolved" either by statutory operation, order of court, or voluntary action on the part of shareholders. Insolvency may result in a form of corporate failure, when creditors force the liquidation and dissolution of the corporation under court order, but it most often results in a restructuring of corporate holdings. Corporations can even be convicted of criminal offenses, such as fraud and manslaughter. However, corporations are not considered living entities in the way that humans are.

Corporations exist as virtual or fictitious persons, granting a limited protection to the actual people involved in the business of the corporation. This limitation of liability is one of the many advantages to incorporation, and is a major draw for smaller businesses to incorporate; particularly those involved in highly litigated trade.

(1) Limited Liability Company (LLC)

A Limited Liability Company (LLC) is a business structure allowed by state statute. LLCs are popular because, similar to a corporation, owners have limited personal liability for the debts and actions of the LLC. Other features of LLCs are more like a partnership, providing management flexibility and the benefit of pass-through taxation.

(2) Partnership

A partnership is the relationship existing between two or more persons who join to carry on a trade or business. Each person contributes money, property, labor or skill, and expects to share in the profits and losses of the business.

(3) Sole proprietorship

A sole proprietorship, also known as a sole trader or simply a proprietorship, is a type of business entity that is owned and run by one individual and in which there is no legal distinction between the owner and the business. The owner receives all profits (subject to taxation specific to the business) and has unlimited responsibility for all losses and debts. Every asset of the business is owned by the proprietor and all debts of the business are the proprietor's. This means that the owner has no less liability than if they were acting as an individual instead of as a business. It is a "sole" proprietorship in contrast with partnerships.

A sole proprietor may use a trade name or business name other than his or her legal name. In many jurisdictions there are rules to enable the true owner of a business name to be ascertained.

In the United States there is generally a requirement to file a doing business as statement with the local authorities.

10.3 Trade Protectionism

Trade protectionism is a type of policy that limits unfair competition from foreign industries. It's a politically motivated defensive measure. However, they adversely affect consumers in general, and the producers and workers in export sectors, both in the country implementing protectionist policies, and in the countries protected against. In the short run, it works. But it is very destructive in the long term. It makes the country and its industries less competitive in international commerce.

10.3.1 Features of Trade Protectionism

There is a broad consensus among economists that protectionism has a negative effect on economic growth and economic welfare, while free trade and the reduction of trade barriers have a positive effect on economic growth. However, liberalization of trade usually results in large and unequally distributed losses and gains, and, in the short run, can cause significant economic dislocation of workers in import-competing sectors.

Protectionism is frequently criticized by economists as harming the people it is meant to help. Mainstream economists instead support free trade. The principle of comparative advantage shows that the gains from free trade outweigh any losses as free trade creates more jobs than it destroys because it allows countries to specialize in the production of goods and services in which they have a comparative advantage. Protectionism results in deadweight loss; this loss to overall welfare gives no-one any benefit, unlike in a free market, where there is no such total loss. According to economist Stephen P. Magee, the benefits of free trade outweigh the losses by as much as 100 to 1. Protectionists believe that there is a legitimate need for government restrictions on free trade in order to protect their country's economic, and therefore political independence.

10.3.2 Basic Methods and Examples

Countries use a variety of strategies to protect their trade. There are four basic methods in practice:

(1) Enacting tariffs that tax imports

That immediately raises the price of the imported goods. They become less competitive when compared to local goods. This method works the best for countries with a lot of imports, such as the United States.

The most famous example is the Smoot-Hawley Tariff of 1930. It was designed to protect farmers from agricultural imports from Europe, which was stepping up farming after the destruction of World War Ⅰ. But by the time the bill made it through Congress, it had slapped tariffs on many more imports. Other countries retaliated. The resultant competitive war restricted global trade. It was one reason for the extended severity of the Great Depression.

(2) Subsidizing local industries

Subsidies come in the form of tax credits or even direct payments. That allows producers to lower the price of local goods and services. This makes the products cheaper even when shipped overseas.

That means subsides work even better than tariffs. This method works best for countries that rely mainly on exports. But sometimes subsidies can have the opposite effect. A good example of this is, once again, in the U. S. agricultural industry. The Agricultural Adjustment Act of 1933 allowed the government to pay farmers not to grow crops or livestock. That would allow their fields to rest and regain nutrients. It also restricted supply. That increased prices. It helped farmers devastated by the Dust Bowl, but made food even more expensive for consumers.

(3) Imposing quotas on imported goods

This method is more effective than the first two. No matter how low a foreign country sets the price through subsidies, it can't ship more goods.

(4) Lowering its currency value

Most textbooks omit the fourth type of trade protectionism because it is subtle. It is a deliberate attempt by a country to lower its currency value. This would make its exports cheaper and more competitive. This method can result in retaliation and start a currency war. One way countries can lower their currency's value through a fixed exchange rate. This is like China's yuan. Another way is by creating so much national debt that it has the same effect, like the U. S. dollar decline.

10.2.3 Advantages and Disadvantages

If a country is trying to grow strong in a new industry, tariffs will protect it from foreign competitors. That gives the new industry's companies time to develop their own competitive advantages. Protectionism also temporarily creates jobs for domestic workers. The protection of tariffs, quotas or subsidies allows domestic companies to hire locally. This benefit ends once other countries retaliate by erecting their own protectionism.

However, in the long term, trade protectionism weakens national industry. Without competition, companies within the industry have no need to innovate. There's no need to improve their competence. Eventually, the domestic product will decline in quality. It will be of lower quality and more expensive than what foreign competitors produce.

Take the execution of trade protectionism in U. S. A for example, the constant job outsourcing is a result of declining U. S. competitiveness. Competition has declined from decades of the United States not investing in education. This is particularly true for high-tech, engineering and science. Increased trade opens new markets for businesses to sell their products. The Peterson Institute for International Economics estimates that ending all trade barriers would increase U. S. income by MYM 500 billion. According to major economist experts, increasing U. S. protectionism will further slow economic growth. It would cause more layoffs, not fewer. If the United States closes its borders, other countries will do the same. This could cause layoffs among the 12 million U. S. workers who owe their jobs to exports.

10.2.4 Solutions to the Problems

Trade protectionism is rarely the answer. High tariffs only protect domestic industries in the short term. But, in the long term, global corporations will hire the cheapest workers wherever they are in the world to make higher profits.

The best solutions are regulations within the agreements that protect against the disadvantages. Environmental safeguards can prevent destruction natural resources and cultures. Labor laws prevent poor working conditions. The World Trade Organization enforces free trade agreement regulations.

Developed economies can reduce their agribusiness subsidies, keeping emerging market farmers in business. They can help local farmers develop sustainable practices, and then market them as such to consumers who value that.

Countries can insist that foreign companies build local factories as part of the agreement. They can require these companies to share technology and train local workers.

Exercises

I. Multiple Choices

1. When a country imposes trade restrictions and no other country reciprocates, which trade agreement should be adopted? ________.

A. Free trade agreement　　B. Unilateral trade agreement

C. Bilateral trade agreement　　D. Multilateral trade agreement

2. For most countries, key protected or subsidized domestic industries are in the following ones except ________.

A. food production　　B. light industry

C. oil　　D. automotive

3. The largest free trade agreement is ________.

A. NAFTA　　B. LLC

C. WTO D. SWTO

4. The biggest disadvantage of multilateral agreements is ________.

A. unique B. complex

C. unpractical D. outdated

5. There are many types of business entities defined in the legal systems of various countries, not including ________.

A. corporations B. vendors

C. sole traders D. limited liability company

II. True or False

1. The largest multilateral agreement is the North American Free Trade Agreement. It is between the United States, Canada and South Africa. ( )

2. Corporations exist as virtual or fictitious persons, granting a limited protection to the actual people involved in the business of the corporation. ( )

3. LLCs are more like a sole proprietorship, providing management flexibility and the benefit of pass-through taxation. ( )

4. Subsidies come in the form of tax credits or even direct payments. That allows producers to lower the price of local goods and services. ( )

5. The free trade agreement will urge some developing countries to complete intellectual property protection. ( )

6. Corporations may be made up of a single person or a group of people, known as sole corporations or aggregate corporations, respectively. ( )

7. Trade protectionism is a type of policy that limits unfair competition from foreign industries. ( )

8. In the long term, trade protectionism strengthens national industry. Without competition, companies within the industry have no need to innovate. ( )

9. If a country is trying to grow strong in a new industry, tariffs will protect it from foreign competitors. ( )

10. Imposing quotas on imported goods would make the country's exports cheaper and more competitive. ( )

III. Questions

1. What are three major types of trade agreements?

2. What are advantages of free trade agreements?

3. Why multilateral trade agreements arc the most difficult to negotiate?

4. Why can the adoption of trade protectionism, in the long run, bring harmful influence on domestic industries?

5. What is a business entity?

References

[1] 杨丽华,董俊英. 贸易实务英语[M]. 北京:首都经济贸易大学出版社,2000.

[2] Contractus. 常见的合同通用条款 [EB/OL]. (2017-12-17). http://blog. sina. com. cn/s/blog/4dae264e0101bck9. html.

[3] 樊红霞,汪奠才. 英文外贸函电[M]. 北京:外语教学与研究出版社, 2007.

[4] Ghlous. purchase CONTRACT 样本[EB/OL]. (2017-12-17). https://wenku. baidu. com/view/5c5c9c98cc22bcd126ff0cc8. html.

[5] 符海菁,张梅英. 外贸英语函电[M]. 北京:高等教育出版社,2014.

[6] Formal Complaint Letter [EB/OL]. (2017-12-20). http://www. letters. org/complaint-letter/formal-complaint-letter. html.

[7] 尹小莹. 外贸英语函电[M]. 西安:西安交通大学出版社,2004.

[8] Sally20108. Inspection claim force majeure and arbitration[EB/OL]. (2017-12-20). https://wenku. baidu. com/view/008d9c5233687e21af45a9dd. html.